IFLA

International Federation of Library Associations and Institutions
Fédération Internationale des Associations de Bibliothécaires et des Bibliothèques
Internationaler Verband der bibliothekarischen Vereine und Institutionen
Международная Федерация Библиотечных Ассоциаций и Учреждений
Federación Internacional de Asociaciones de Bibliotecarios y Bibliotecas
国际图书馆协会与机构联合会

الاتحاد الدولي لجمعيات ومؤسسات المكتبات

IFLA Publications 147

IFLA Public Library Service Guidelines

2nd, completely revised edition

Edited by
Christie Koontz and Barbara Gubbin

De Gruyter Saur

IFLA Publications
edited by Sjoerd Koopman

Library of Congress Cataloging-in-Publication Data

IFLA public library service guidelines. -- 2nd, completely rev. ed. / edited by Christie Koontz and Barbara Gubbin.
    p. cm. -- (IFLA publications, ISSN 0344-6891 ; 147)
  Rev. ed. of: The public library service / prepared by a working group chaired by Philip Gill on behalf of the Section of Public Libraries. 2001.
  Includes bibliographical references and index.
  ISBN 978-3-11-023226-4 (alk. paper)
  1. Public libraries--Standards. 2. Public libraries--Administration. 3. Public libraries--Aims and objectives. I. Koontz, Christie. II. Gubbin, Barbara. III. International Federation of Library Associations and Institutions. Section of Public Libraries. Public library service. IV. Title: Public library service guidelines.
  Z678.85.I575 2010
  027.4--dc22
                            2010021182

ISBN 978-3-11-023226-4
e-ISBN 978-3-11-023227-1
ISSN 0344-6891

Bibliographic information published by the Deutsche Nationalbibliothek
The Deutsche Nationalbibliothek lists this publication in the Deutsche Nationalbibliografie; detailed bibliographic data are available in the Internet at http://dnb.d-nb.de.

Walter de Gruyter GmbH & Co. KG, Berlin/New York
Data conversion and typesetting by Dr. Rainer Ostermann, München
Printing and binding by Strauss GmbH, Mörlenbach

∞ Printed on permanent paper
The paper used in this publication meets the minimum requirements of American National Standard – Permanence of Paper for Productions and Documents in Libraries and Archives
ANSI/NISO Z39.48-1992 (R1997)

Printed in Germany

www.degruyter.com

Contents

4   Collection development

5   Human resources

6   The management of public libraries

7   The marketing of public libraries

Appendices

Preface

This publication revises the Guidelines for public libraries published in 2001. It was drafted by a working group made up of members of the Committee of the IFLA Section of Public Libraries.

The public library is the dynamic and premiere community access point designed to proactively respond to a multitude of ever-changing information needs. These guidelines are framed to provide assistance to library and information professionals in most situations, to assist them in better developing effective services, relevant collections, and accessible formats within the context and requirements of the local community. In this exciting and complex information world it is important for library and information professionals in search of knowledge, information and creative experience to succeed. We hope these guidelines will facilitate this search, ultimately enhancing the learning power and quality of life of people in the community the libraries serve.

We are grateful to all those past and present that commented on and contributed to this work as it has progressed since its inception in 1973. Special gratitude is expressed to the IFLA Section of Public Libraries members who provided practical examples to illustrate the text, and member John Lake for his editing skills. Thank you to Nicole Stroud, library and information professional and former Florida State University graduate student, for her assistance with editing the book and her contribution to the new section (digital collection development.) We would also like to acknowledge those who contributed to other new sections: Janet Lynch Forde (information literacy); Monika Antonelli (green libraries); Lauren Mandel (E-government services); Laura Brenkus (human resources materials); editor, Christie Koontz (marketing).

The continued interest shown in this publication over many years is evidence of the demand for guidelines for public libraries that reflect the changed information world in which libraries continually operate. We trust that these guidelines will be relevant to public libraries at varying stages of development in the 21st century and can continue to help library and information professionals meet the challenges they face daily. It is in that belief that this revised publication is offered to all those involved in the development of public libraries throughout the world.

Editors, Christie Koontz and Barbara A.B. Gubbin

Introduction

The previous 2001 edition included examples of service provision from around the world as does this edition. These are not intended to be comprehensive or necessarily the most outstanding instances of service provision. These illustrate the text with some snapshots of what is happening in public libraries in different countries and to provide a glimpse of imaginative solutions to specific challenges. We realize that these are very selective and many more examples could be used that would be equally relevant. These do demonstrate what is being done throughout the world to match the public library service to the needs of its customers in a local context. We have also included website addresses for some of the initiatives, to provide access to more detailed information about them. Relevant resources are now appended to each chapter. A list of IFLA publications is interspersed amongst chapters as well as summarized at the end of the book. Two new appendices include the Queensland Standards and Guidelines for Public Libraries and the Update of the IFLA Manifesto 2009.

In the last few years the rapid and very exciting developments in information technology (IT) revolutionized the way in which information is collected, displayed and accessed. The synergy between information and communications technology (ICT) is allowing access to information in ways hardly imaginable when the Guidelines were published in 1986 as well as in 2001. The speed of change accelerates and continues to do so. There are few sectors of activity not affected and the public library, for which the provision of information is a primary role, is facing the challenge of radical changes in all aspects of its organisation and service delivery.

Many public libraries are responding to the challenge of the electronic revolution, taking the opportunity to develop services in new and exciting ways. But for people to take advantage of the opportunities ICT presents there is a basic need for literacy, computer skills and a reliable telecommunications network. The risk of a growing gap between the information rich and the information poor continues. This gap is not just an issue between countries at different stages of development but also between groups and individuals within countries.

Public libraries face an exciting opportunity to help to bring everyone into this global conversation and to bridge what is often called 'the digital divide'. They are achieving this by providing information technology for public access, by teaching basic computer skills and by participating in programmes to combat illiteracy. However, to fulfill the principle of access for all, they must also continue to maintain services that provide information in different ways, for example, through print or the oral tradition. These are likely to remain of vital importance for the foreseeable future. While becoming the gateway to the electronic information world should be a key objective for the public library, every effort must be made not to close other doors through which knowledge and information can be provided. These factors present public libraries with a major challenge and their response will determine the continuing viability of the public library service. The recommendations are framed with these issues in mind.

1

The mission and purposes of the public library

'The public library, the local gateway to knowledge, provides a basic condition for lifelong learning, independent decision-making and cultural development of the individual and social groups.'

(IFLA/UNESCO Public Library Manifesto, 1994)

1.1   Introduction

This chapter is a general statement on the mission (as defined and mandated by IFLA/UNESCO 1994, Appendix 1) and purpose of the public library. The key issues reviewed are developed in greater detail in later chapters.

1.2   Defining the public library

Public libraries are a world-wide phenomenon. Libraries occur in a variety of societies, in differing cultures and at different stages of development. Although the varied contexts in which libraries operate inevitably result in differences in the services provided, and the way those services are delivered, libraries normally have characteristics in common, which can be defined as follows.

A public library is an organisation established, supported and funded by the community, either through local, regional or national government or through some other form of community organisation. It provides access to knowledge, information, lifelong learning, and works of the imagination through a range of resources and services and is equally available to all members of the community regardless of race, nationality, age, gender, religion, language, disability, economic and employment status and educational attainment.

1.3   The purposes of the public library

The primary purpose of the public library is to provide resources and services in a variety of media to meet the needs of individuals and groups for education, information and personal development including recreation and leisure. They have an important role in the development and maintenance of a democratic society by giving the individual access to a wide and varied range of knowledge, ideas and opinions.

▸ The Council for Public Libraries initiated a new vision statement for Finnish public libraries, "The Library is a meeting
place of people and ideas. Library: Inspiring, Surprising, Em-
powering."
▸ The Guidelines and Standards for Queensland Public Libraries were designed to improve current procedures and provide
achievable goals for the public libraries in Queensland, Australia. The standards are seen as a guide towards achieving
'best practice' for those responsible for the management of
public library services (see Appendix 6).
<http://www.slq.qld.gov.au/info/publib/build/standards.>

1.3.1   Education

'Supporting both individual and self conducted education as well as formal education at all levels.'

(Manifesto)

The need for an agency available to all, which provides access to knowl-edge in printed and other formats such as multimedia and Internet sources, to support formal and informal education, has been the reason for the foundation and maintenance of most public libraries and re-mains a core purpose for the public library. Throughout their lives people require education either at formal institutions, for example, schools, colleges and universities, or in a less formal context related to their employment and daily life. Learning does not end with the com-pletion of formal education but is, for most people, a lifelong activity. In an increasingly complex society people will need to acquire new skills at various stages of their life. The public library has an important role in assisting this process.

The public library should provide material in the appropriate media to support formal and informal learning processes. It should also help the customer to make use of these learning resources effectively as well as providing facilities that enable people to study. The ability to access information and make effective use of it is vital to successful education and, where possible, public libraries should co-operate with other educational organisations in teaching the use of information resources. Where adequate library facilities exist to support formal education the public library should complement these.

The public library should also actively support literacy and information literacy campaigns and training, as literacy is the key to education and knowledge and to the use of libraries and information services. Newly literate people need easy access to appropriate information materials and services to maintain and develop their skills.

In some countries the need for educational development is seen to be paramount and the focus of public libraries is to support formal education. There are, however, a variety of ways in which public libraries can support both formal and informal education. How this is achieved will depend on the local context and the level of available resources.

▸ In Singapore the stated mission for public library service is "to provide trusted, accessible, globally-connected, library and information service so as to promote a knowlegeable and engaged society."
▸ In South Africa, where many people have inadequate living space and no electricity to enable them to study, public libraries have prioritised provision of the basic facilities, artificial light, and tables and chairs.
▸ In some countries, libraries are required to fulfil multi-functions e.g., of both public and school libraries. In England, a smaller branch library is combined with a larger school library and located within a leisure facility. In the USA, college and public libraries are sometimes combined, such as the Central Library in San Jose, CA and Harris County Library in Tomball, TX. <http://www.hcpl.net/location/tomball-college-community-library>
▸ In Amazonas State, Venezuela, where there are few school libraries, rural libraries concentrate on providing support for students and teachers.

▸ In Barcelona province, Spain, some library services offer support to distance learning students from the Open University in Catalonia.

▸ In the State of Queensland, Australia, the Gold Coast City Council Mobile Library visits geographically isolated primary schools.

▸ Norwegian libraries established quality-controlled internet sites with indexed links to resources suitable for education on different age levels. <http://detektor.deichman.no/>

▸ Large urban libraries like the Queens Borough Public Library in New York, USA and the Copenhagen Public Library in Denmark offer customers specially designed learning centres in their buildings. These centres include staff that provides instructional assistance with educational materials and computers.

▸ Russian Astrakhan Regional Children's Library communicates with young readers online. Incoming questions are referred to appropriate departments with the goal of processing requests within 24 hours. Those residing far from the library can now receive necessary books or magazines.
<http://www.goroganin.info/index.php?id_a=733>

▸ *Entrelibros* (Between books) is a *net* of customers and books promoted by the Autonomous Government of Extremadura, Spain. <http://plataformadelectores.org>

▸ In the State of Queensland, Australia, public libraries provide homework resources and support to upper primary and secondary school children through organised homework clubs in libraries. Electronic homework support is also available. <http://netlinks.slq.qld.gov.au/>

1.3.2   Information

'The public library is the local centre of information making all kinds of knowledge and information readily available to its users.'

(Manifesto)

It is a basic human right to be able to have access to and an understanding of information, and there is now more information available than ever before in the world's history. As a public service open to all, the public library has a key role in collecting, organizing and exploiting information, as well as providing access to a wide range of information sources. The public library has a particular responsibility to collect local information and make it readily available. It also acts as a memory of the past by collecting, conserving and providing access to material relating to the history of the community and of individuals. In providing a wide range of information the public library assists the community in informed debate and decision-making on key issues. In collecting and providing information the public library should, wherever possible, cooperate with other agencies to make the best use of available resources.

The rapid growth in the volume of available information and the continuing technological changes, which have radically affected the way information is accessed, have already had significant effect on public libraries and their services. Information is very important to the development of the individual and of society, and information technology gives considerable power to those able to access and use it. Despite its rapid growth it is not available to many of the world's populations, and the gap between the information rich and the information poor continues to widen in some areas. Sources of widespread public information such as television broadcasting, telephone, and other mobile web based services, educational institutions and public libraries are taken for granted in developed countries. In developing countries, however, such infrastructure is seriously deficient, and this hinders individual ability to gather information and solve problems. The Internet promises improvements to internal communications in and among developing countries. Public libraries play a role in this and must bridge that gap by providing widespread public access to the Internet (when technologically possible) as well as continuing to provide information in traditional formats. Public libraries should recognise and exploit the opportunities provided by the continued and increasing developments in information and communications technology. Public libraries continue to provide an important access point to online information services.

▸ Some public libraries in South Africa provide space for information kiosks and telecentres.

▸ Rural multi-purpose community telecentres established in 5 African countries (Benin, Mali, Mozambique, Tanzania and Uganda) provide access to modern information and communication tools.

▸ The public library in Memphis, TN, USA, includes non-traditional information such as genealogy records, a small business centre, and job opportunities listings. Other city libraries in the USA, in Dallas, TX and San Francisco, CA, offer local, state and national government information.

- Open access Internet points are available in public libraries in Estonia.
- Australia's Gold Coast City Council regularly hosts a two day "Techno Expo" providing customers opportunities to explore and learn all about gadgets, tools and concepts which incorporate the latest technologies.

1.3.3   Personal development

'Providing opportunities for personal creative development.'

(*Manifesto*)

The opportunity to develop personal creativity and pursue new interests is important to human development. To achieve this, people need access to knowledge and works of the imagination. The public library can provide access, in a variety of different media, to a rich and varied store of knowledge and creative achievement, which individuals cannot acquire on their own behalf. Providing access to major collections of the world's literature and knowledge including the community's own literature, is a unique contribution of the public library and still a vitally important function. Access to works of the imagination and knowledge is an important contribution to personal education and meaningful recreational activity. Libraries must extend traditional bibliographic instruction of how to search the catalogue and use print reference tools, to training customers on how to use computers to locate information and evaluate the quality of that information.

The public library can also make a fundamental contribution to daily survival and social and economic development by being directly involved in providing information to people in developing communities; for example, basic life skills, adult basic education and AIDS awareness programmes. In communities with a high illiteracy rate the public library should provide services for non-literates and interpret and translate information where necessary. Basic education regarding how to use the library and its services should also be provided.

- The Rural Audio Libraries of Mali distributed information on hygiene, health, animal husbandry and other topics relevant to people's daily lives. These reached 146 villages, and collective listening sessions were organised.

▸ In Bolivia, local libraries are venues for a variety of activities, such as health campaigns, classes in nutrition, mother and baby and youth clubs.

▸ Employment information centres are offered in some USA libraries. Job seekers can get information about work opportunities and use a variety of media to help prepare for job applications and interviews. These projects can forge links between library staff and the regional government workforce offices.

▸ A key objective for library services in rural areas of Venezuela was to improve the quality of life of small farmers with limited resources by providing agriculture and animal husbandry information.

▸ Crandall Public Library in Glen Falls, NY, USA, provided a Health Information Centre complete with a telephone hotline available to answer the public's health questions.
<http://www.crandalllibrary.org/programs/programs-consumerhealth.php>

▸ London libraries offer a range of books and other resources to help people improve literacy, numeracy and information technology skills.
<http://www.londonlibraries.org/servlets/llr/skillsforlife/all>

1.3.4   Children and young people

'Creating and strengthening reading habits in children from an early age.'

(Manifesto)

The public library should attempt to meet the needs of all groups in the community regardless of age and physical, economic or social circumstances. However, it has a special responsibility to meet the needs of children and young people. If children can be inspired by the excitement of knowledge and by works of the imagination at an early age, they are likely to benefit from these vital elements of personal development throughout their lives, both enriching them and enhancing their contribution to society. Children can also encourage parents and other adults to make use of the library. It is also important that young people who experience difficulty in learning to read should have access to a library to provide them with appropriate material (see Paragraphs 3.4.2 and 3.4.3).

▸ The Central Public Library in Novouralsk, Russia developed a mobile information service focusing on youth entitled, "I am looking for an answer", with the objective of providing immediate information online.
<http://www.publiclibrary.ru/readers/services/virtual-spravka-child.htm>

▸ "Chitatel.ru or (Reader.ru)" created by the Centralized System of Municipal Libraries, Omsk, Russia targets youth. The online menu offers options to find some 'interesting books and quotes by renowned authors.'

▸ Centralized Library System of Pskov, Russia, through customer research, identified teenagers as becoming increasingly nonconformist. The library's website, "ABC of 'neformal'"
<http://www.bibliopskov.ru/neformal/index.htm> explains the essence of teen subcultures, philosophies, psychologies and lifestyles.

1.3.5   Public libraries and cultural development

An important role of the public library is providing a focus for cultural and artistic development in the community and helping to shape and support the cultural identity of the community. This can be achieved by working in partnership with appropriate local and regional organisations, by providing space for cultural activity, organizing cultural programmmes and by ensuring that cultural interests are represented in the library's materials. The library's contribution should reflect the variety of cultures represented in the community. It should provide materials in the languages spoken and read in the local community, and support cultural traditions. Libraries should strive to employ staff who speak the languages of the community served.

▸ Librarians working in Amazonas, Venezuela, were trained to act as intermediaries between different cultures as many people living in the rural communities may only speak and understand their native language.

▸ The Newark Public Library, NJ, USA, developed the Charles Cummings New Jersey Information Center focusing on local and state history in partnership with the New Jersey Historical Commission.

▸ The central libraries of the Republic of Croatia offer library service for all ethnic minorities including books in their mother language, relevant exhibitions, literary and other cultural events, and interlibrary lending to supplement local ethnic needs.

▸ Australian Gold Coast City Council Libraries celebrate "Cultures on the Coast" with monthly programmes of multicultural interest that are organised and delivered by diverse groups ultimately raising cultural awareness within the community.

1.3.6   The social role of the public library

The public library has an important role as a public space and meeting place. This is particularly important in communities where there are few places for people to meet. It is sometimes called 'the drawing room of the community.' Use of the library for research, education, and leisure interests, brings people into informal contact, providing a positive social experience. Library facilities should be designed and built to foster social and cultural activities which support community interests.

▸ Denmark libraries acknowledge while the traditional use of the Internet for information searching is still the norm, use of the Internet as a communication platform is growing exponentially. A project modelling '23 Things' of the USA Public Library of Charlotte & Mecklenberg
<http://www. plcmc.org/> demonstrates the need for the development of library staff competencies within the social networking web 2.0 area.
<http://splq.info/issues/vol41_2/06.htm>

▸ Entresse Library, Finland is located in a shopping mall. It is a multicultural library with staff as heterogeneous as its customers. Targeted groups include teenagers and immigrants. Librarians walk through the facility with mobile phones and laptops to provide services to these sometimes difficult to reach populations.
<http://english.espoo.fi//default.asp?path=32373;37337;4 5340;37077;70550;83170 >

▸ Library 10 is a branch of the Helsinki, Finland, city library, located in the city centre providing innovative services to customers such as the *Audio-editing* and *Rehearsal* rooms, where customers can practice or record music. The *Stage* functions as a venue for cultural performances, discussions, and other exhibits. <http://www.lib.hel.fi/en-GB/kirjasto10/>

1.4   An agency for change

In carrying out its role in these key areas the public library is acting as an agency for social and personal development and can be a positive agency for change in the community. By providing a wide range of materials to support education and by making information accessible to all, the public library can bring economic and social benefits to individuals and to the community. It contributes to the creation and maintenance of a well–informed and democratic society and helps to empower people in the enrichment and development of their lives and that of the community in which they live.

The public library should be aware of the issues that are being discussed within the community and provide information that will inform that debate.

1.5   Freedom of information

'Collections and services should not be subject to any form of ideological, political or religious censorship, nor commercial pressures.'
(Manifesto)

The public library should be able to represent all ranges of human experience and opinion, free from the risk of censorship. In some countries a Freedom of Information Act (such as the United Stated enacted) will help to ensure these rights are maintained. Librarians and governing bodies should uphold these basic human rights and resist pressure from individuals and groups to limit the material available in the public library.

▸ In Denmark, libraries encourage citizens to join in political debate and take an active part in democracy through the project, 'The library as democratic hothouse.' In the city of Herning, the library cooperates with local journalists and politicians to create a debating culture which is active on both the Internet and via discussion within the physical space. <http://splq.info/issues/vol42_1/04.htm>

> ▸ The Australian Library and Information Association believes library and information services have particular responsibilities in supporting and sustaining the free flow of information and ideas. <http://www.alia.org.au/policies/free.access.html>

1.6   Access for all

A fundamental principle of the public library is that its services must be available to all and not directed to one group in the community to the exclusion of others. Provision should be made to ensure services are equally available to minority groups who for some reason are not able to use the mainstream services, for example, linguistic minorities, people with physical and sensory disabilities or those living in remote communities who are unable to reach library buildings. The level of funding, development of services, the design of libraries and opening hours should be planned with the concept of universal access as a basic principle (see chapter 3 'Meeting the needs of the customers' and discussion of some national laws which require library compliance for service to disabled populations.)

The development of collections should also be based on the principle of access for all and include access to formats appropriate to specific client groups, for example, Braille and talking books for visually impaired people. Information and communications technology (ICT) should be used to allow access to the library's collections and those of other information sources publicly available on the Internet, from within the library or from remote sites.

1.7   Local needs

Public libraries are locally based services for the benefit of the local community and should provide community information services. The services and collections they provide should be based on local needs, which should be assessed regularly. Without this discipline the public library will get out of touch with those it is there to serve and will, as a result, not be used to its full potential. Librarians should, therefore, be aware of the changes in society arising from such factors as social and economic development, demographic change, variations in the age structure, levels of education, patterns of employment and the emergence of other educational and cultural providers (see chapter 6.10, Environmental scanning).

1.8   Local culture

The public library should be a key agency in the local community for the collection, preservation and promotion of local culture in all its diversity. This can be achieved in a variety of ways, for example, the maintenance of local history collections, exhibitions, storytelling, publishing of items of local interest and developing interactive programmes on local themes. Where the oral tradition is an important method of communication the public library should encourage its continuation and development.

- ▸ Village Reading Rooms in Botswana served as centres for storing Setswana literature and promoting the Setswana language and for the promotion of culture where discussion groups, traditional songs, dances and meetings are organised.
- ▸ In Singapore, an Asian Library Services Unit provides services in the local languages: Chinese, Malay and Tamil.
- ▸ In Cuba, libraries may act as venues for poets as well as encourage research into and the conservation of peasant oral traditions.
- ▸ "Village Libraries" in India provide a platform for documenting traditional knowledge. Books are published which are written by villagers.
- ▸ "Memoria Viva" is a compilation of information about the civil war in Spain housed in Bacelona's libraries.
- ▸ Hämeenlinna city library in Finland founded a local history wiki 'Häme-Wiki,' and teaches locals how to edit the wiki. The project is a combination of *home town reflections* and learning about social media.
  <http://www.hamewiki.fi/wiki/Etusivu>
- ▸ State Library of Queensland, Australia, provides local studies' standards to maintain and provide access to collections which document the historical development of the local community.
  <http://www.slq.qld.gov.au/info/publib/policy/guidelines/eight>
- ▸ Russian Arkhangelsk Regional Scientific Library provides a portal created as a regional network information resource dedicated to popularizing knowledge about the history and culture of the Arkhangelsk region. All information is concentrated in the thematic sections: "Folklore", "Literature", "Folk arts and crafts," "Theatre", "Visual Arts", "Music", "Architec-

ture", "Traditions and customs". In each section there are lists of persons and biographical information, along with updated links to Internet resources and reference lists of literature.
<http://www.cultnord.ru/>

▸ The National Library of the Republic of Karelia is a participant in a project for the creation of a distributed system which identifies book monuments in Russia. The project is initiated by the Russian State Library under the federal target programme "Culture of Russia."
<http://library.karelia.ru/cgi-bin/monuments/index.cgi>

▸ In Spain local history digitalization projects funded by the Ministry of Culture include the open repository OAI / PMH, and the Biblioteca Virtual de Prensa Historica (Historial Press Virtual Library).
<http://prensahistorica.mcu.es/es/estaticos/contenido.cmd?pagina=estaticos/oai>

▸ RODA, Repositorio de Objetos digitales y de aprendizaje. RODA is a project offering collections of printed historical matter housed in the Caceres Public Library, containing a total of 118 303 colour images, primarily the legacy of Antonio Rodriguez and Mary Monino Brey.
<http://roda.culturaextremadura.com>

1.9   The cultural roots of the public library

It is important to the long-term success of the library that it should be based on the culture, or cultures, of the country or area in which it operates. It is less likely to succeed if the form and structure of the public library are introduced from a country or area with a very different cultural background. Library management can identify services needed through community surveys of actual and potential customers, public meetings, focus groups and other methods to gather broad-based community input.

▸ The Centralized Library System Kemerovo created "BiblioVita" to facilitate customers' personal growth and self-knowledge, while secondarily augmenting appreciation of the depth and breadth of library services.
<http://www.kemcbs.com/index.php?page=bv>

> ‣ The Jacksonville Public Library System, FL, USA,
> <http://jpl.coj.net/res/sites/historyfl.html> offers collections
> highlighting the history and heritage of the state and special
> populations such as the African American residents of the
> area.

1.10   Libraries without walls

In developing policies to fulfill the role and purpose of the public library the emphasis should be on the services it provides. In meeting
the needs of its community the public library will provide a range of
services, some of which (for example, large collections of printed material), can be most effectively delivered from a library building. However, there will be many circumstances where it is more effective to
provide the service beyond the walls of the library. Examples will vary
in different societies but the principle of planning library development
from a service rather than a building perspective is important in all
public library policy development. The provision of services using information and communications technology (ICT) also presents exciting opportunities to take library and information services direct to the
home and the workplace.

A variety of forms of transport are used to deliver services to
sparsely populated areas. The provision of library and information services to people unable to visit a library due to physical or sensory disability or lack of transport, for example, ensures that access to these
services is available to all at their home or workplace regardless of their
circumstances. These 'mobile library' services are sometimes housed in
a van or bus, and as stated provide not only books, but additionally
multimedia and increasingly often, Internet access. When these provide
the latter the vehicles are sometimes named 'infomobiles.'

> ‣ The public library service in Chile developed a variety of mo-
> bile services including bookmobiles, book boats, book boxes,
> backpacks and bicycles. The services offer books and cultural
> activities for all ages and travel across diverse terrains. They
> also serve rest homes, hospitals and prisons.
> ‣ In Catalonia, Spain a network of mobile libraries provides
> books, multimedia and Internet access.
> ‣ The mobile library of Leppävirta, Finland is a library and com-
> munity multi-service-centre. There is an Internet workstation,

healthcare information, stamps for sale, and customers can have medicine, shopping, laundry or heavier mail transported to their home by the mobile library. Customer research prior to building the mobile unit indicated what kind of services the elderly desired.

▸ Gold Coast City Council, Australia, was the first mobile library of its kind with three extendable pods providing technology centres for adults and children.
<http://www.goldcoast.qld.gov.au/library/t_library.aspx?pid=7731>

▸ Bibliobus is the name for the modern mobile library centre, usually providing updated book collections, providing Internet access, specialised databases and audiovisual facilities for local educational and cultural events. The mobile library allows residents of remote rural areas to access information and educational services, helping overcome the digital divide. Bibliobuses are successfully utilised in the UK, USA, Germany, Finland, and Russia.
<http://www.library.ru/3/focus/bibliobus.php>

▸ In Ethiopia, donkeys "power" bookmobiles, taking books to outlying villages.
<http://www.ethiopiareads.org/programs/mobile>

1.11   Library buildings

Library buildings play an important part in public library provision. These should be designed to reflect the functions of the library service, be accessible to all in the community and be sufficiently flexible to accommodate new and changing services. They should be located close to other community activities, for example, shops and cultural and transportation centres. Wherever possible the library should also be available for community use, for example, for meetings and exhibitions and in larger buildings for theatrical, musical, audiovisual and media performances. A well used public library will make a significant contribution to the vitality of an urban area and be an important learning and social centre and meeting place, particularly in scattered rural areas. Librarians should, therefore, ensure that library buildings are used and managed effectively to make the best use of the facilities for the benefit of the whole community.

> ▸ The Turku main library in Finland embodies 21st century archi-
> tecture which enhances new innovative concepts for the li-
> brary services provided.
> <http://www.turku.fi/Public/default.aspx?nodeid=12503&cul
> ture=en-US&contentlan=2>
> ▸ Hjørring Central Library is described as Denmark's premiere
> example of a 21st century public library, and the 'most spec-
> tacular and ultimate library place to be.'
> <http://splq.info/issues/vol41_4/07.htm>
> ▸ The new public library building in Kolding, Denmark is situated
> close to the city centre with a unique view 'to the lake and
> former castle Koldinghus.' With its transparency, open spaces
> and light wooden interiors it represents the minimalist con-
> tinuation of the Scandinavian library style.
> <http://www.librarybuildings.info/denmark/kolding-library>
> ▸ The (more or less) bookless Danish children's library is de-
> signed with children very much in mind as well as within the
> framework of today's knowledge society.
> <http://splq.info/issues/vol41_3/07.htm>
> ▸ The Russian Library Association provides a portal, "Library
> buildings: architecture, design, organisation of space"
> <http://rba.okrlib.ru/biblioteki/fotogalereya/> offering images
> of libraries, and building design.

1.12   Resources

To fulfill its roles satisfactorily the public library must have adequate
resources, not just when it is established but also on a continuing basis,
embracing emerging technologies as these enter society to enable it to
sustain and develop services that meet the needs of the local community. This means it should provide materials and services in all formats, up-dated regularly to meet the changing needs of groups and individuals, including newly-published and replacement materials and
new information technologies as available and which can be supported.
It should also provide adequate levels of staff with appropriate training
and sufficient funds to support whatever methods of service delivery
are needed for it to meet its vital role in the community. Subsequent
chapters identify and provide an understanding of resources for optimal public library service.

1.13   Value of public libraries

It is acknowledged that public libraries provide great value to their communities. Value is often defined by what materials and services libraries provide to the communities. In the past public libraries primarily offered access to printed information, and served as a public social and physical meeting place in the community. In the digitized age the role and value of public libraries has become enhanced by the advent of new information technologies. These may include workstations, increased available bandwidth, and provision of computer training. In some communities today, public libraries are the sole provider of free access to the Internet.

The value of public libraries is often discussed around these service provisions. There have been numerous studies that provide economic modelling (see chapter 6 'The Management of public libraries' for some quantifiable performance indicators.)

▸ A USA library developed an integrated communications public awareness campaign to promote the value of its services via cable television, public service announcements, Web sites, and an interactive TV programme where viewers may "talk" to a live librarian.

▸ The first comprehensive Australian study of the value which public libraries bring to their communities is entitled "Libraries Building Communities." The report includes views and ideas gathered from over 10 000 people via online and print surveys and focus groups.
<http://www.slv.vic.gov.au/about/information/publications/policies_reports/plu_lbc.html>

Resources

Aabø, S. (2005). "The role and value of public libraries in the age of digital technologies." *Journal of Librarianship and Information Science* vol. 37(4), pp. 205-211. (http://lis.sagepub.com/cgi/content/abstract/37/4/205 accessed 1/01/2010).

Berk & Associates, Inc. (2005). The Seattle Public Library Central Library: Economic benefits assessment. (http://www.spl.org/pdfs/SPLCentral_Library_Economic_Impacts.pdf accessed 30/12/2009)

Bertelsen, E., and Cranfield, V. (2001). *Act Regarding Library Services*. Copenhagen: Danish National Library.
(http://www.bs.dk/publikationer/english/act/pdf/Act_reg__library_ser.pdf accessed 1/01/2010)

Česko. (2003). *Law No. 257/2001 Coll. of 29 June 2001 on Libraries and Terms of Operating Public Library and Information Services (Library Act)*. Prague: National Library of the Czech Republic.
(http://knihovnam.nkp.cz/english/sekce.php3?page=04_Leg/02_LibAct.htm &PHPSESSID=3658c047e024d207dc073e8bc945a775 accessed 1/01/2010).

Cologne city. (n.d.). World literature: Library literature in Cologne.
(http://www.stadt-koeln.de/5/stadtbibliothek/bibliotheken-archive/literaturwelt/ accessed 1/01/2010).

Cologne Library Association. (n.d.). Cologne Library Association minibib (kiosk in the park). (http://www.foerderverein-stadtbibliothek-koeln.de/ accessed 1/01/2010)

Freedominfo.org. (n.d.). Freedominfo.org: The online network of freedom of information advocates. (http://freedominfo.org/ accessed 1/01/2010).

Goethe-Institut. (n.d.). Sau Paulo – Wissen – Bibliothek – Goethe-Institut: favela projects in Brasil. (http://www.goethe.de/ins/br/sap/wis/bib/deindex.htm accessed 1/01/2010).

Governo do Estado do Paraná. (n.d.). Projects of the Regional Government of Paraná.
(http://www.cidadao.pr.gov.br/ accessed 1/01/2010).

Hage, C. (2004). *The public library start up guide*. Chicago: American Library Association.

IFLA. (1995). *IFLA/UNESCO Public Library Manifesto*, The Hague: IFLA.
(http://www.ifla.org/VII/s8/unesco/manif.htm accessed 1/01/2010).

IFLA. (1999). IFLA/UNESCO School Library Manifesto.
(http://www.ifla.org/en/publications/iflaunesco-school-library-manifesto-1999 accessed 1/01/2010).

IFLA. (2002). The IFLA Internet Manifesto.
(http://www.ifla.org/publications/the-ifla-internet-manifesto accessed 1/01/2010).

Kekki, K., Wigell-Ryynänen, H. (2009). Finnish Public Library Policy 2015. National strategic areas of focus. Publications of the Ministry of Education.
(http://www.minedu.fi/OPM/Julkaisut/2009/kirjasto_ohjelma.html?lang=en accessed 1/01/2010).

Larsen, J., and Wigell-Ryynänen, B. (2006). *Nordic public libraries in the knowledge society*. København : Danish National Library Authority.

(http://www.bs.dk/publikationer/english/nnpl/pdf/nnpl.pdf
accessed 1/01/2010)

Latimer, K., and Niegaard, H. (2007). *IFLA library building guidelines: Developments & reflections*. München: K.G.Saur.

Levin, Driscoll & Fleeter. (2006). Value for money: Southwestern Ohio's return from investment in public libraries.
(http://9libraries.info/docs/EconomicBenefitsStudy.pdf
accessed 1/01/2010)

Library Council of New South Wales, J.L. Management Services, and State Library of New South Wales. (2008). *Enriching Communities: The Value of Public Libraries in New South Wales*. Sydney: Library Council of N.S.W.

Maine State Library. (n.d.). Library use value calculator.
(http://www.maine.gov/msl/services/calculator.htm accessed 1/01/2010).

Mattern, S. (2005). *Public places, info spaces: creating the modern urban library*. Washington: Smithsonian Books.

MD Brasil Ti & Telecom. (n.d.). MD Brasil Ti & Telecom: Sao Paulo, Brazil favela „Monte Azul" (www.monteazul.com.br accessed 1/01/2010) LINK BROKEN 5.25.2010

Pestell, R., and IFLA Mobile Libraries Round Table. (1991). *Mobile library guidelines*. Professional report #28. The Hague: IFLA. (Currently being revised)

Romero, S. (2008). *Library Architecture: Recommendations for a comprehensive research project*. Barcelona: Colegio de Arquitectos de Catalunya.

SirsiDynix (n.d.). SirsiDynix Institute.
(http://www.sirsidynixinstitute.com
accessed 1/01/2010)

State Library of Queensland. (n.d.) Standards and guidelines.
(http://www.slq.qld.gov.au/info/publib/build/standards
accessed 1/01/2010)

Thorhauge, J. (2002). *Danish Library Policy: A Selection of Recent Articles and Papers*. Biblioteksstyrelsen. Copenhagen: Danish National Library Authority.
(http://www.bs.dk/publikationer/english/library_policy/pdf/dlp.pdf
accessed 1/01/2010).

Urban Libraries Council and The Urban Institute. (2007). Making cities stronger: Public library contributions to local development.
(http://www.urban.org/uploadedpdf/1001075_stronger_cities.pdf
accessed 1/01/2010)

Buildings

Bisbrouck, M. et al (2004). *Libraries as places: Buildings for the 21ˢᵗ century*. IFLA Publications Series 109. Munchen: K.G. Saur.

Bryan, C. (2007). *Managing facilities for results: optimizing space for services*. Chicago: American Library Association.

Dewe, M., (2006). *Planning public library buildings: concepts and issues for the librarian*, Aldershot, England: Ashgate.

Hauke, P. (2009). *Bibliotheken bauen und ausstatten*. Bad Honnef: Bock + Herchen. (http://edoc.hu-berlin.de/oa/books/ree8FL3pymekE/PDF/25Gh3UywL6dIY.pdf)

IFLA Section on Library Buildings and Equipment, *Intelligent library buildings: proceedings of the tenth seminar of the IFLA Section on Library Buildings and Equipment, The Hague, Netherlands, 24–29 August, 1997*, Marie-Françoise Bisbrouck and Marc Chauveinc (eds), IFLA Publication – 88, Munich, K. G. Saur, 1999

Koontz, C.M. (1997). *Library Facility Siting and Location Handbook*. Westport, CT: Greenwood Press.

Latimer, K., and Niegaard, H. (2007). *IFLA library building guidelines : developments & reflections*. Munich: K. G. Saur.

Niegaard, H., Schulz, K., and Lauridsen, J. (2009). *Library Space: Inspiration for building and design*. Copenhagen, Danish National Library Authority.

2

The legal and financial framework

'The public library is the responsibility of local and national authorities. It must be supported by specific legislation and financed by national and local governments. It has to be an essential component of any long-term strategy for culture, information provision, literacy and education.'

(*IFLA/UNESCO Public Library Manifesto*, 1994)

2.1   Introduction

Public libraries are a community agency providing access at the local level to a range of knowledge and information for the benefit of the individual and society as a whole. In order to maintain the level of service required to fulfill their functions public libraries should be supported by legislation and sustained funding.

2.2   The public library and government

There are many different models of the relationship between public libraries and government. Equally, the laws that govern their activities and funding arrangements are varied and complex. In different countries, provinces, regions, states or municipalities are, either in whole or in part, responsible for library services. As public libraries are a locally based service, local government is often the most appropriate place in the government structure. However, in some countries public libraries are provided at a regional or state level and the national library sometimes has responsibility for providing the public library service. There are instances of two or more levels of government co-operating in the provision of the service.

▸ The Estonian Public Libraries Act (1998) detailed the responsibilities of each level of government. It states that the public library is established by the local government body, and that the county or city library is responsible for the co-ordination of library service, interlibrary loans and book mobiles. The local authority is responsible for employees' wages but the funding of library materials is shared between the local authority and the state.

▸ State Library of Queensland, Australia produced guidelines and standards for Queensland public libraries designed to enhance current practices and to provide achievable goals for public libraries in Queensland (see Appendix 6). <http://www.slq.qld.gov.au/info/publib/build/standards>

▸ Association of Regional Library Consortium (ARBICON) in Russia was established to coordinate library activities and improve the quality of services by modernizing the management of resources through the merger of library consortia. <http://www.arbicon.ru/>

2.2.1   Alternative structures

In some countries, although the local authority has nominal responsibility for the public library, it does not have the required funds. Therefore, non-governmental organisations or private foundations undertake the practical operation of the public library services. However, to ensure sustained development and its role in the information network, the public library should be closely related to and funded by the appropriate level of government. The eventual aim should be to bring public libraries into the formal government structure operating under national legislation and with appropriate levels of funding.

▸ Argentina established public libraries and provided these through non-governmental organisations, or organised communities regulated by national legislation.

2.2.2   National information policies

In order to make the most effective use of available library and information resources, and take full advantage of the opportunities offered by the development of digital information sources, many countries are developing national information policies. Public libraries should be a key element in such policies and public librarians should ensure they are fully involved in their development.

▶ The CePSE, [Central de Préstec I Serveis Especials] Delivery Center and Special Support Services, focuses its mission on providing services and a professional collection, to ultimately improve the practices and procedures of public and school libraries in Catalonia, Spain. <http://cultura.gencat.cat/cepse>

2.2.3   E-Government services

E-Government (E is for electronic) strives to engage citizenry in government in a user-centred manner, and thus develop quality government services and delivery systems that are efficient and effective via new technologies. User-centred E-Government suggests that governments will provide services and resources tailored to the actual service and resource needs of users, including citizens, residents, government employees, and others. A key issue for libraries is that citizen-centred E-Government services may be tasked to local libraries. Public libraries are often identified as optimal partners for provision of E-Government services as they are the most logical public point of access. Additional funds from government should be sought for provision of these services. Adequate equipment, connections, and trained staff with appropriate expertise are necessary.

It is a public library's role to provide public service. Yet in the E-Government scenario public libraries are sometimes not prepared or forewarned of government closures and elimination of in-person citizen services, with these being transferred to the web. Therefore preparation and policies must be in place as to if or how the library will provide these government services within its mission and available resources. It is recommended to examine staff expertise and current government partnerships to assure optimal preparation is in place for this seemingly inevitable trend occuring in communities.

▶ The Pasco Public Library Cooperative in FL, USA, has a dedicated E-Government librarian, along with special sections of the library's website that focus on E-Government. For example, the "Online Government Services" page offers most-requested,

local government, city and municipality, state, and federal government services. <http://pascolibraries.org/>
- ▸ The New Jersey State Library, USA, developed a website to assist residents through difficult economic times. The website offers work, financial, housing, health, parental, and senior tools. Each tool offers links to further E-Government information related to that topic. <http://gethelp.njlibraries.org/>

2.3   Public library legislation

The establishment of public libraries should be based on legislation, which assures their continuance and place in the government structure. Public library legislation takes various forms. In some countries or regions the legislation is specific to public libraries whereas in others it is part of wider legislation which includes different types of libraries. Public library legislation is also varied in its provisions. It can be simple, allowing the establishment of public libraries but leaving standards of service to the level of government directly responsible for the library, or more complex, with specific detail on what services should be provided and to what standard.

Because governmental structures vary so much in different countries the form and detail of public library legislation is also likely to vary significantly. However, legislation governing public libraries should state which level of government is responsible for provision and how they should be funded. It should also place them in the framework of libraries in the country or region as a whole.

- ▸ Mexico and Venezuela have specific public library legislation whereas in Colombia and Brazil legislation on information services includes references to public libraries.
- ▸ The Finnish Library Act (1998) stipulates that the public library should be provided by the municipality, either independently or in co-operation with other public libraries, that public libraries should co-operate with other types of libraries and that the municipality should evaluate the library and information services that it provides (see Appendix 2).
- ▸ The Constitution of the Republic of South Africa 1996 provided the constitutional framework for the provision of library and information services in South Africa. It lists 'libraries other than national libraries' as an area of exclusive provincial legis-

lative competence. It is, therefore, a provincial responsibility to develop the legislative framework in which library and information services can be provided.

▸ In Armenia, local authorities have responsibility for the financing and maintenance of public libraries. The Law on Local Self-Government defined their obligations for maintaining and developing public libraries.

▸ In the Russian Federation, there are two laws relating to libraries at the federal level, the Library Act and the Legal Deposit Copy Act. These were not concerned solely with public libraries though most of the Library Act is devoted to them.

▸ The Italian Constitution gives Regions the control of public libraries established by municipalities and provinces. Some Regions issued Library Acts in order to regulate co-operation between libraries and other information, documentation, cultural and educational agencies and to set quality standards.

▸ Guidelines on library legislation and policy in Europe were issued by the Council of Europe and EBLIDA (European Bureau of Library, Information and Documentation Associations).

2.3.1   Related legislation

Public libraries are subject to a range of legislation apart from the specific legislation relating to them. This can include legislation on financial management, data protection, health and safety and staff conditions and there are many other examples. Library managers should be aware of all legislation affecting the operation of the public library.

They should also be aware of global trade negotiations, which can result in policies and agreements, which could have a serious impact on public libraries. In such cases librarians should take every opportunity to bring the effect of such policies on public libraries to the notice of the public and politicians.

2.3.2   Copyright

Copyright legislation, especially that relating to electronic publications, is of particular importance to public libraries. It is constantly subject to amendment and review and librarians should keep up-to-date with the legislation in relation to all media. Librarians should promote and support copyright legislation, that achieves an equitable balance between the rights of creators and the needs of users.

> ▸ In the Czech Republic the library association SKIP, acting on its own initiative, participated in the preparation of copyright legislation. After discussions with the Ministry of Culture and the Cultural Committee of the Czech parliament, changes beneficial to libraries were introduced.

2.3.3   Public lending right

In some countries, public lending right legislation has been introduced which provides a payment to authors and others involved in the creation of a book, related to its provision in, and loan from, public libraries. It is important that funds for payment of public lending right should not be taken from libraries' funds for the purchase of materials. However, public lending right (PLR), if separately funded, does provide support for authors without affecting public libraries' budgets. In some schemes it can also provide useful statistics on the loans of books by specific authors. Librarians should participate in the development of public lending right schemes to ensure they are not financed from library budgets.

> ▸ The Danish government provides funds for PLR payments to Danish authors, translators, artists, photographers and composers who contribute to a printed work. This is defined as cultural support.
> <http://www.bs.dk>
> ▸ In Australia, the PLR is administered by the Department of the Environment, Water, Heritage and the Arts to make payments to eligible Australian creators and publishers on the basis that income is lost from the availability of their works in public lending libraries. The PLR supports the enrichment of Australian culture by encouraging the growth and development of Australian writing and publishing.
> <http://www.arts.gov.au/books/lending_rights/public_lending_right_-_guidelines_for_claimants>

2.4   Funding

Adequate levels of funding are crucial to the success of a public library in fulfilling its roles. Without sufficient levels of funding over the long-term it is impossible to develop policies for service provision and make the most effective use of available resources. This can be seen in a number of examples: a new library building without adequate funds to maintain it, collections of new books with no money for their replacement and computer systems without funds to maintain and update them. Funding is required not only when a public library is established, but should also be sustained on an assured and regular basis and funding needs made known to community customers.

▸ A USA library offers a calculator to answer, "What is your library worth to you? How much would you pay out-of-pocket for your library services?"
<http://www.maine.gov/msl/services/calculator.htm>
▸ The Queensland State Government via the State Library of Queensland outlines the obligations of the provision of a free public library.
<http://www.slq.qld.gov.au/__data/assets/pdf_file/0017/12 2048/SLQ_-_Service_Level_Agreement_-_September_2008. pdf>
▸ Vladimirskaya Region Universal Scientific Library developed a manual "Paid Services in the Municipal Libraries."
<http://www.library.vladimir.ru/load/metod_03.doc>   Examples of annual reports are published on the library website.
<http://slib.admsurgut.ru/inf13.htm>
▸ Central City Children's Library of Kemerovo conducts annual public meetings with readers
<http://www.okrlib.ru/chitatelyam/biblioteka_kak_ona_est/>
to report the work and accomplishments of the libraries, introduce upcoming activities, and share customer data. These reports help substantiate library expenditures.

2.4.1   Priorities

A public library and the services it provides is a long-term investment on behalf of the community and should be funded appropriately. It is recognised that even in the wealthiest of societies it may not be possible to provide appropriate levels of funding for every service requirement. It is vitally important, therefore, that service development should be conducted on a planned basis with clear priorities. This process is necessary whatever level of funding is available to the library service. To determine strategic planning and the maintenance of agreed priorities, written policy statements should be developed for services. These should be reviewed at regular intervals and revised where necessary.

2.4.2   Partnerships & collaborations

No public library, however large and well funded, can meet all the needs of its customers on its own. Participation in partnerships, collaborations, and networks with other libraries and related organisations, and the provision of access to other sources of information, enables the public library to satisfy the information needs of its users by increasing the range of available resources.

> ▸ Queens Borough Public Library, NY, USA, is collaborating with the Brooklyn Children's Museum and the San Francisco, CA, Exploratorium, to bring museum exhibits into the children's room. The project *Science in the Stacks* seeks to better facilitate hands-on learning of science, math and technology, and make available relevant materials to young customers and their parents in a community where as many as 97 languages are spoken.
> <http://www.queenslibrary.org/>

2.4.3   Sources of funding

A number of sources of funding are used to finance public libraries but the proportions of funding from each source will vary depending on local factors in each country.

The primary sources are:

- taxation at local, regional or central level
- block grants from central, regional or local level.

Secondary sources of income may include:

- donations from funding bodies or private individuals
- revenue from commercial activities, e.g., publishing, book sales, sale of works of art and handicrafts
- revenue from customer fees, e.g., fines
- revenue from charges to customers for individual services, e.g., photocopying and printing facilities

- sponsorship from external organisations
- lottery funds for specific initiatives.

2.4.4 Charging the customer

The *IFLA/UNESCO Public Library Manifesto* states: 'The public library shall in principle be 'free of charge'. Charging customers for services and membership should not be used as a source of revenue for public libraries, as it makes the ability to pay a criterion in determining who can use a public library. This reduces access and therefore breaches the fundamental principle that the public library should be available to all. It is recognised that in some countries subscriptions to join the library or charges for specific services are levied. Such charges inevitably deny access to those unable to afford them. They should be seen as an interim situation and not as a permanent feature of public library funding.

It is common in some countries to ask customers to pay a fee or fine when keeping an item after it is due for return to the library. This is sometimes necessary to ensure that items are kept in circulation and not retained for a long time by one customer. The fine should not be set at a level that would deter anyone from using the library. Charges are also sometimes levied for personalized services, for example photocopying or use of a printer. These charges should also not be set at a level which will deter the customer.

2.4.5 Funding for technology

Public libraries must, whenever possible, make use of the new technologies to improve services and provide new ones. This means a considerable investment in various kinds of electronic equipment, and a reliance on this equipment for the delivery of services. To continue to perform effectively equipment should be upgraded and replaced. This has significant funding consequences, and a plan for the replacement and upgrading of technological equipment should be developed.

▸ State Library of Queensland, Australia, outlines a framework for the efficient and effective use of technology as an integral feature of public library services.
<http://www.slq.qld.gov.au/__data/assets/pdf_file/0006/16 2726/SLQ_-_Queensland_Public_Library_Standards_and_Guide lines_-_Technology_Standard_-April_2010.pdf

2.4.6   External funding

Librarians should be proactive in seeking external sources of funding for the public library. However, they should not accept funding from any source if, by so doing, the fundamental status of a public library as an agency available to all is compromised. Commercial organisations, for example, may offer funding with conditions which might prejudice the universal nature of the services provided by the public library. All proposals should be recorded and agreed upon by all parties before enactment.

▸ The public library in Tarragona, Spain, received funding from business enterprises in the city to run a commercial and economic information service.
▸ The Chicago Public Library Foundation in the USA is a non-profit organisation that supports the collections and programmes of the Chicago Public Library. The Foundation has provided start-up funding for new programmes, such as technology, and expanded Sunday and evening service hours. <http://www.chicagopubliclibraryfoundation.org/about/>

2.5   The governance of the public library

Public libraries should be governed by a properly established body made up largely of representatives of the local community including those elected either to the local council or to the library board. Library committees and boards should have rules of procedure and their proceedings should be open to the general public. They should meet on a regular basis and publish agenda, minutes, annual reports and financial statements. Normally the governing body will be responsible for matters of policy rather than the day-to-day operation of the library. In all cases the chief librarian should have direct access to the meetings of the governing body of the library and work closely with it. Policy documents should be made available to the public and, where possible, steps should be taken to involve local citizens in the development of the public library.

Public librarians must be fully accountable both to their governing bodies and local citizens for their actions by providing reports, holding public meetings and through consultation. They must also maintain the highest professional standards in carrying out their duties and in advising the governing body. Although the final decisions on policy will be taken by the governing body and the librarian, ways should be sought to involve the local citizens who are the actual or potential library customers. The concept of a 'library charter', which identifies and publicises the level of service the public library provides, has been developed in some countries (see Appendix 3 for a sample charter). This establishes a 'contract' between the public library and the customers. Library charters have more credibility if they are developed in consultation with customers.

▸ A Finnish university library developed technology planning documents for better managing e-services; e-media, and e-collections. Topics include policies for use of equipment; training; telecommunications and bandwidth; filtering access to the web; standards for technology i.e., computers per capita, and equipment replacement plans.
<http://www.docstoc.com/docs/29302907/Joensuu-University-Library>

▸ State Library of Queensland, Australia, outlines standards and guidelines for a minimum set of operational services that enable the community effective access to library facilities and the services and collections they offer (see Appendix 6).

2.6   The administration of the public library

Public libraries should be well managed and administered. The administration of a public library should be directed towards improving the quality of service to the customers and not as an end in itself. It should be efficient and accountable. To get best results the administrative and management staff of a large public library service should be multidisciplinary, involving staff with specialist skills, for example, librarians, accountants, public relations officers and systems managers. It may also be necessary to draw on the expertise of staff of the parent authority or other related organisation in certain areas, for example, lawyers, payroll and pensions staff.

2.7   Publicity and promotion

Public libraries operate in an increasingly complex society, which makes many calls on people's time and attention. It is important, therefore, that libraries publicise their presence and the range of services they provide. Publicity ranges from simple techniques, like signs on library buildings stating what they are, and leaflets advertising opening hours and services, to more sophisticated methods like marketing programmes and the use of websites to promote the library's services and activities (see Chapter 7 'The marketing of public libraries').

Resources

Bertot, J., Jaeger, P., and McClure, C., "Citizen-centered e-government services: benefits, costs, and research needs." *Proceedings of the 2008 international conference on Digital government research.*
(http://portal.acm.org/citation.cfm?id=1367832.1367858
accessed 01/01/2010).

IFLA. (n.d.) Public libraries section: Acts on library services.
(http://www.ifla.org/V/cdoc/acts.htm accessed 1/01/2010).

IFLA Section of Public Libraries. (1998). *The public library as the gateway to the information society: the revision of the IFLA guidelines for public libraries, proceedings of the IFLA/UNESCO Pre-Conference Seminar on Public Libraries, 1997.* The Hague: IFLA.

Karppinen, D., and Genz, M. (2004). *National information policies: improving public library services?* Thesis (M.S.)--Florida State University
(http://etd.lib.fsu.edu/theses/available/etd-08232004-225005/
accessed 01/01/2010)

Kretzmann, J., and Rans, S. (2005). *The Engaged Library: Chicago Stories of Community Building.* Chicago, Ill: Urban Libraries Council.
(http://www.urbanlibraries.org/associations/9851/files/ULC_PFSC_Engaged
_0206.pdf accessed 1/01/2010)

Maine State Library. (n.d.). Library use value calculator.
(http://www.maine.gov/msl/services/calculator.htm accessed 1/01/2010).

Online Computer Library Center, Inc. (2008). From awareness to funding: a study of library support in America.
(http://www.oclc.org/reports/funding/fullreport.pdf)

Sarkodie-Mensah, K. (2002). *Helping the difficult library patron: new approaches to examining and resolving a long-standing and ongoing problem.* New York: Haworth Information Press.

Susman, T. (2002). *Safeguarding our patrons' privacy: what every librarian needs to know about the USA PATRIOT Act & related anti-terrorism measures : A satellite teleconference cosponsored by American Association of Law Libraries, American Library Association, Association of Research Libraries, Medical Library Association, Special Libraries Association.* Washington, DC: Association of Research Libraries.

United States Department of Justice. (n.d.). Freedom of Information Act (FOIA) (http://www.justice.gov/oip/ accessed 1/01/2010).

Urban Libraries Council, and The Urban Institute. (2007). Making cities stronger: Public library contributions to local development. (http://www.urban.org/uploadedpdf/1001075_stronger_cities.pdf accessed 1/01/2010)

Walker, J., Manjarrez, C. (2003). *Partnerships for free choice learning: public libraries, museums, and public broadcasters working together.* Washington DC: Urban Institute.

World Intellectual Property Organization. (n.d.). Collection of laws for electronic access (CLEA). (http://www.wipo.int/clea/en/ accessed 1/01/2010).

Woodward, J. (2007). *What every librarian should know about electronic privacy.* Westport, CT: Libraries Unlimited.

Yarrow, A., Clubb, B., Draper, J., and IFLA Public Libraries Section. (2008). *Public Libraries, Archives and Museums: Trends in Collaboration and Cooperation.* Professional reports, #108. The Hague: IFLA. (http://www.ifla.org/en/publications/ifla-professional-reports-108)

3

Meeting the needs of the customers

'The services of the public library are provided on the basis of equality of access for all, regardless of age, race, sex, religion, nationality, language or social status.

To ensure nation wide library coordination and cooperation, legislation and strategic plans must also define and promote a national library network based on agreed standards of service.

The public library network must be designed in relation to national, regional, research and special libraries as well as libraries in schools, colleges and universities.

Services have to be physically accessible to all members of the community. This requires well situated library buildings, good reading and study facilities, as well as relevant technologies and sufficient opening hours convenient to the users. It equally implies outreach services for those unable to visit the library.

The library services must be adapted to the different needs of communities in rural and urban areas.'

(*IFLA/UNESCO Public Library Manifesto*, 1994)

3.1   Introduction

To be successful in fulfilling its goals the public library service must be fully accessible to all its customers. Customer is the term used primarily throughout the Guidelines (just as user, patron or client might be) to optimise consideration of public library non-users as potential customers. Also implicit in the term customer, individuals have expressed wants and needs to be identifed and met.

Customers ultimately have the choice of participating in public library service offered – or not. Therefore, any limitation of access, whether deliberate or accidental, will reduce the ability of the public library to fully achieve its primary mission and role of meeting the library and information needs of the community served. The following are important elements in delivering an effective public library service:

- identifying potential customers
- analysing customers' needs
- developing services to groups and individuals
- introducing customer care policies
- promoting library use education
- co-operating and sharing resources
- developing electronic networks
- ensuring access to services
- providing library buildings.

3.2   Identifying potential customers

The public library has to aim to serve all citizens and groups. An individual is never too young or too old to use a library onsite or online.

The public library has the following potential customer groups.

- People at all ages and at all stages of life:
  - children
  - young adults
  - adults
  - elderly

- Individuals and groups of people with special needs:
  - people from different cultures and ethnic groups including indigenous people
  - people with disabilities, e.g., physical, blind and partially sighted, hearing impaired
  - housebound people
  - institutionally confined people, e.g., in hospitals, prisons
  - people lacking knowledge of library services

- Institutions within the wider community network:
  - educational, cultural and voluntary organisations and groups in the community
  - the business community
  - the governing body of the parent organisation, e.g., local authority.

As resources are limited in even the wealthiest society it is not always possible to serve all customers to the same level. The library must establish priorities based on an analysis of actual and potential customer needs and related to their access to alternative services.

3.3   Analysing needs within the community

It is important to establish who uses and who does not use the library service. It is also necessary to collect and analyse data that identifies those needs of individuals and groups within the community that can be met by the public library. (see chapter 6.10 'Management tools').

3.4   Services to customers

The public library must provide services based on an analysis of the library and information needs of the local community. In planning services, clear priorities must be established and a strategy be developed for service provision in the medium to long term. Services should be developed for identified target groups and only provided if such groups exist in the local community.

The services of the library should not be subject to any form of ideological, political, religious or commercial pressure. Services must be able to adjust and develop to reflect changes in society, for example, variations in family structures, employment patterns, demographic changes, cultural diversity and methods of communication. They should take account of traditional cultures as well as new technologies, for example, support for oral methods of communication as well as making use of information and communication technology. In some countries the services that the public library must provide are defined in library legislation.

3.4.1   Service provision

Public libraries provide a range of services, both within and delivered from the library, and in the community, to satisfy customers' needs. The library should facilitate access to its services for all, including those who have difficulty accessing services due to physical or mental disabilities. The following services should be as easily accessible as possible to the customers through a variety of formats, media, and via the Internet including:

- loan of books and other media
- provision of books and other materials for use in the library
- information services using print and electronic media
- readers' advisory services including reservation services
- community information services
- library use education including support for literacy programmes
- programming and events
- modern communication tools such as blogs, cell phone messaging, and social networking tools used for both reference services and public relations.

This is not an exhaustive list but an indication of some of the key services of the public library. The range and depth of provision will depend on the size of the library and the community it serves. Every library should aim to be an active participant in one or more networks, which will give the customer access to a wide range of materials and services, however small the access point. Service provision should not be confined to the library building but also taken directly to the customer where access to the library is not possible. In providing services, both within the library and beyond, use should be made of information and communications technology as well as the printed word. A list of some of the resources the library should provide is detailed in Paragraph 4.3.1.

3.4.2   Services to children

By providing a wide range of materials and activities, public libraries provide an opportunity for children to experience the enjoyment of reading and the excitement of discovering knowledge and works of the imagination. Children and their parents should be taught how to make the best use of a library and how to develop skills in the use of printed and electronic media.

Public libraries have a special responsibility to support the process of learning to read, and to promote books and other media for children. Research indicates that if children do not develop the reading and library habit as a child, this will be unlikely to emerge as an adult. The library then must provide outreach, special events for children, such as storytelling and activities related to the library's services and resources. And children should be encouraged to read, develop information literacy skills, and use the library from an early age. In multilingual countries books and multimedia for children should be available in their mother tongue.

▸ In France, some public libraries are co-operating with Health Services for Children to organise programmes for parents and their children while they are waiting for medical consultation. These are aimed at children aged birth to 3 years old, encouraging parents to read aloud to their children and visit the public library.

▸ In Bucharest, Romania, the city library offers summer programmes, run by volunteers, aimed at children aged 11 to 14 whose parents are at work.

▸ In the Netherlands, groups of people over age 50 were trained by the public library to read to children in schools, kindergarten and child care centres.

▸ In the State of Queensland, Australia, a range of activities for children is provided by the public library, including sessions for under fives, their parents and caregivers, storytelling, class visits, library orientation, reading groups, Internet training and homework clubs.

▸ The library service in Johnson County, Kansas, USA, provided 'Books to Grow' kits for pre-school through to first grade. Each kit has a theme and contains five books, one audio tape, one video tape and one activity folder.

▸ In Singapore, 41 childrens libraries for children under age 10 were established in co-operation with a local grassroots organisation, with collections of 10,000 items, full Internet services and a story-telling room. The funding came from the Library Board and the local organisation.

▸ Many libraries in the Nordic countries offer an incentive to visit the library by giving a gift book to parents and children on their first visit to the maternal and child health centre.

▸ *"Ten Commandments for the future children's library"* is a new report offering recommendations and suggestions for library services to children in Denmark.
<http://splq.info/issues/vol41_3/04.htm>

▸ The *"Young people's dream library"* report indicates the young in Denmark desire a library which accepts them as they are. This dream library is also well-planned and easily accessible. Young people hope librarians will accept their youthful behaviour, and be within reach when they need assistance.
<http://splq.info/issues/vol40_1/04.htm>

▸ The Centralised System of Municipal Libraries in Omsk, Russia implemented the cultural-educational project "World of Books for Kids," with the goal of enhancing a positive attitude to-

wards reading amongst pre-schoolers, their parents, care-givers, and pre-school educational institutions.
<http://www.lib.omsk.ru/csmb.php?page=pp33>
▸ Central City Children's Library of A.P. Gaydar, Moscow, offers information to parents of, and children with, disabilities.
<http://www.gaidarovka.ru/index.php?option=com_content&task=category&sectionid=6&id=87&Itemid=292>

3.4.3   Services for young adults

Young people between childhood and adulthood develop as individual members of society with their own culture. Public libraries must understand their needs and provide services to meet them. Materials, including access to electronic information resources, that reflect their interests and culture should be provided. In some cases this will mean acquiring materials that represent youth culture, in a variety of media that are not traditionally part of a library's resources, for example, popular novels, book and television series, music, DVDs, teenage magazines, posters, computer games, and graphic novels. It is important to enlist the help of young people in selecting this material to ensure that it reflects their interests. In larger libraries this material, with appropriate furniture, can form a special section of the library. This will help them to feel that the library is for them and help to overcome a feeling of alienation from the library, which is not unusual among this age group. Relevant programmes and talks to young adults should also be provided (see *IFLA Guidelines for Library Services for Young Adults*).

▸ In Hamburg, Germany, young adults help to select and buy media stock for the young adults' library in a project called EXIT. The selections reflect their cultural background. The youth organised and gained sponsorship for their own Internet café. <http://www. buecherhallen.de>
▸ In Queensland, Australia, public library staff receive specialist training in working with young adults. The training covers customer care, programming ideas and how to run teenage advisory groups and homework clubs. In conjunction with local teenagers, many libraries have developed youth spaces.
▸ In Singapore a library aimed at people aged 18–35 has been established in the heart of the shopping area. Focus groups helped to define the profile of the collection and design the library.

> ▸ In the USA, the Standards for Public Library Services to Young Adults in Massachusetts (MA) <http://www.masslib.org/yss/REVISIONFeb051.pdf> advises providing reference services for homework assistance, personal, career and college information – using telephone and online referral. Reference librarians at the Haverhill Public Library in MA use instant messaging, texting, calling, and emailing to better communicate with youth. <http://www.haverhillpl.org/Services/askalibrarian.html>

3.4.4   Services for adults

Adults will have different requirements of an information and library service related to the variety of situations they will encounter in their studies, employment and personal life. These requirements should be analysed and services be developed on the outcome of that analysis. They should include support for:

- lifelong learning
- leisure time interests
- information needs
- community activities
- cultural activity
- recreational reading.

Services meeting these needs should also be available to children and young adults.

3.4.5   Lifelong learning

The public library supports lifelong learning, working with schools and other educational institutions to help students of all ages with their formal education. The challenge of providing educational support provides an opportunity for public libraries to interact and network with teachers and others involved in education. The public library should also provide a range of materials on a variety of topics which will allow people to follow their interests and support their formal and informal education. It should also provide materials to support literacy and the development of basic life skills. In addition the library must provide study facilities for students who have inadequate or no access to these facilities in their homes.

The expansion of distance learning is having an impact on the public library. Distance learners, studying at home, are likely to make use of their local library as their primary source for material. Many will require access to the Internet which the public library should provide. Public libraries play an increasingly important role within the educational network and should provide space and access to materials to meet this demand.

▸ South Dublin County Library Service, Ireland, provides self-learning facilities for adults, including computer-based learning and audio and video-based language-learning materials. The aim is to provide a neutral and supportive environment in which individuals can learn at their own pace.

▸ Two libraries in Oklahoma, USA, sponsor discussion groups for new adult readers with grants from the National Endowment for the Humanities. The group reads one book at a time, usually a classic, and then discusses it with the help of a group facilitator.

3.4.6   Leisure time interests

People need information to support their leisure time interests, and meeting this need by a range of resources in a variety of formats is another key role of the public library. Public libraries must be aware of the cultural, social and economic changes in the community and develop services that are sufficiently flexible to adjust to these changes. The public library should also help to preserve the culture, history and traditions of the local community and make these readily available.

The public library, by organizing activities and exploiting its resources, should encourage artistic and cultural development in people of all ages. The library is also an important social centre for individuals and groups to meet both formally and informally. This is of special importance in communities where other meeting places are not available.

3.4.7   Information services

The rapid development of information technology has brought a vast amount of information within reach of all those with access to electronic media. Information provision has always been a key role of the public library and the ways in which information can be collected, accessed and presented have changed radically in recent years. The public library has a number of roles in providing information:

- providing access to information at all levels
- collecting information about the local community and making it readily accessible, often in co-operation with other organisations
- training people of all ages in the use of information and the associated technology
- guiding customers to the appropriate information sources
- providing opportunities for disabled people to have independent access to information
- acting as a gateway to the information world by making it accessible to all, thus helping to bridge the gap between 'the information rich' and 'the information poor'.

The dramatic development of the Internet has been largely unstructured and uncontrolled. The vast amount of information that can be accessed via the Internet is of variable quality and accuracy and a key role of the librarian is to guide customers to accurate information sources, which will meet their requirements.

▸ In Horsens, Denmark, the library staffs an information booth supplying governmental, regional and local information, directing people to the right public department, and offering help with completion of government forms. Consumer questions are also answered. Both printed material and the Internet are used to deal with enquiries.
<http://www.bibliotek.horsens.dk>

▸ The Comfenalco Public Library in Medellin, Colombia, offers a website with up-to-date information about the city, including institutions, personalities, cultural events and procedures related to public services. It also publishes a series of guides on questions most frequently asked by customers.
<http://www.comfenalcoantioquia.com/sil>

▸ Libraries and Borger.dk (translated: Citizen.dk) is a national campaign promoted by Denmark's public libraries which encourages the public to access an established Internet portal. The website is designed to help people better manage their personal communications with public authorities.
<http://splq.info/issues/vol42_3/07.htm.>

3.4.8   Services to community groups

The public library should be at the centre of the community if it is to play a full part in its activities. It should, therefore, work with other groups and organisations in the community. This will include departments of government and local government, the business community and voluntary organisations. An analysis of the information needs of these bodies should be conducted, and services be provided to meet these needs. This will not only help the organisations involved but will also demonstrate, in a practical way, the value of the public library to people in the community who are likely to have some influence on the future of the library service. Many public libraries, for example, provide an information service to local government politicians and staff, giving a practical demonstration of the value of the public library.

▸ Essex County Library, United Kingdom (UK), created websites for voluntary organisations. The library makes a small charge for this service at below the commercial level.

▸ Grant funds were used in Arizona, USA, to provide a computer lab in the library for use by children and adults from the Hualapai tribe.

▸ In the West Midlands region of United Kingdom (UK), a project (INTER-ALL) supported by funding from the European Regional Development Fund provides information to small businesses. Learning and information centres are being established in 13 libraries in the region, supported by 15 full-time positions.

3.4.9   Services to special customer groups

Potential customers who, for whatever reason, are unable to use the regular services of the library have a right to equal access to library services. In the United Kingdom, all libraries must comply with the Disability Discrimination Act and in the United States, the Americans with Disabilities Act. The library should in all cases strive to establish ways of making library material and services accessible to these customers. Library managers should be familiar with local ordinances to be in compliance. These will include:

- special transport, e.g., mobile libraries, book-boats and other forms of transport to serve those living in isolated areas
- services taken to the home of those people who are housebound

- services taken to factories and industrial premises for employees
- services for those confined in institutions, e.g., prisons and hospitals
- special equipment and reading materials for those with physical and sensory disabilities, e.g., hearing impaired and visually impaired people
- special materials for people with learning difficulties, e.g., easy-to-read materials and multimedia
- services for immigrants and new citizens to help them to find their way within a different society and to provide access to media of their native culture
- electronic communication, e.g., the Internet, electronic databases and other online resources.

Services for people with special needs can be enhanced by the use of new technology, for example, speech synthesizers for the visually impaired, online access catalogues for those in isolated areas or unable to leave their home, and connections to remote sites for distance learning. Mainstream service provision, for example, online public access catalogues (OPACs) can often be adapted to meet the needs of those with physical and sensory disabilities. Those who can benefit the most from technological developments are often the least able to afford the investment needed. Innovative schemes should, therefore, be developed by the public library to exploit the new technology in order to make services available to as many people as possible.

Services for ethnic groups in the community and for indigenous peoples should be developed in consultation with the group concerned. They are likely to include:

- the employment of staff from the group in the library
- collections including the native literature of the group and reflecting the oral tradition and non-written knowledge of the people
- the application of special conditions, developed in conjunction with local people, to culturally sensitive material.

▸ The Information Centre at Odense University Hospital is one of the oldest patient libraries in Denmark. The centre offers unique multi-disciplinary services for patients and relatives as well as information on health and specific illnesses. <http://www.ifla.org/files/lsn/newsletters/66.pdf>
▸ Denmark's Integration Exploratory for Ethnic Minorities focuses on library services for these populations, incorporating

theories of *"empowerment and new audience development"* in order to implement new library services and improve existing ones.
<http://www.odense.dk/web/eksperimentarium/english.aspx>

▸ The section entitled "Mercy" on the website of the Central Public Library of Novouralsk, Russia, is a collection of information and best practices of libraries and various other organisations serving persons with disabilities.
<http://www.publiclibrary.ru/readers/mercy/about.htm>

▸ The Oslo Public Library in Norway maintains a tailor made web-service for language minorities in 14 languages. It contains information about libraries, culture, Norwegian society, how to learn the Norwegian language and identifies organisations for ethnic minorities. <http://bazar.deichman.no/>

▸ Public libraries in Croatia carry out literacy and reading programmes such as bibliotherapy and logobibliotherapy (preparing more easily read materials) for people with disabilities.

3.4.10   The library in the community

Library services are not bound by the walls of the library. Services can be provided or accessed in key locations throughout the community. Providing services where people congregate enables the library to connect with those who cannot easily visit the library.

▸ Library services have been provided at Metro stations in Santiago, Chile.

▸ Beach libraries serve vacationers in Catalonia, Spain and in Portugal during the summer months.

▸ Many forms of transport are used to deliver library services. Bookmobiles are common in many countries. There are book boats in Norway and Indonesia, where bicycles and pedicabs are also used. Donkeys in Peru transported laptop computers as well as books, camels were utillzed in Kenya and donkey-carts in Ethiopia. Mopeds are used to deliver books to the home or office in Apeldoorn, Netherlands.

▸ In parts of South Africa library services have been supplied to informal settlements or squatter areas with no infrastructure. This is done in a variety of ways, for example, from car boots, steel cabinets in clinics, cargo containers, under a tree or provided by individuals or shops to other members of the community. Block loans are sometimes provided to schools and old people's homes. Storytelling and school project information is sometimes available at after-care centres for children unable to go the library.

‣ In Colombia, steel cabinets containing about 300 books, a bench and a space for a billboard were provided in places where people congregate. They opened for about two hours a day.

‣ In Manassas, VA, USA, a mall store-front housed the state's first electronic library. It offered (free to county residents) no books but rather computing and technology courses and virtual library services.

3.4.11 Reading promotion and literacy

Reading, writing and the ability to use numbers are basic prerequisites to being an integrated and active member of society. Reading and writing are also the basic techniques needed for making use of new communication systems. The public library should support activities that will enable people to make the best use of modern technology. It should support other institutions that are combating illiteracy and promoting media competence. It can achieve this by:

• promoting reading
• providing appropriate materials for those with poor literacy skills
• working with other agencies in the community involved in combating illiteracy
• participating in campaigns to combat illiteracy and improve numeracy
• organising events to promote an interest in reading, literature and media culture
• promoting and providing training in the use of computer technology
• promoting awareness of new developments in the media market
• helping people to find the information they need in the appropriate format
• co-operating with teachers, parents and other contact persons to help new citizens acquire the necessary educational skills that will help them to manage their lives in the new context.

The public library provides a range of creative literature and can use promotional techniques to bring its variety and range to the attention of its customers. It can also organise interactive programmes that enable customers to exchange views about books that they have read.

> ▸ An interactive programme developed in Wandsworth, England, uses multimedia software to encourage readers to experiment with their reading and engage in dialogue about books they have read.
> ▸ The Book Bites project developed by The Libraries of Copenhagen, Denmark, in cooperation with a number of publishers, sends out a section of a novel via e-mail to approximately 1000 subscribers, so that after one week, each has received the entire first chapter.
> <http://www.bibliotek.kk.dk/bibliotekerne/biblioteksudvikling /projekter/projekt- bogbidder-til-alle>
> ▸ Offaly and Limerick County Libraries, Ireland, in partnership with literacy students, tutors, local literacy organisers and the National Adult Literacy Agency, are active agents in literacy provision. They make a wide range of books and other materials available to adult literacy students and their tutors and generally promote a reading culture.
> ▸ In Singapore, the library works with a self-help group, training women who are learning English. Classes are held in the libraries, which support the programme by providing the resources needed.
> ▸ Comfenalco library in Medellin, Colombia, has a weekly page in the main city newspaper that includes reviews and comments on books for children.
> ▸ The "Project Love of Reading" in Denmark, attempts to stimulate bilingual children's joy of reading, by inspiring them to select favourite books from different genres and levels of reading, while simultaneously offering library use instruction. This project also strives to position the library as an active participant in the local society and neighbourhood.
> <http://www.bibliotek.kk.dk/bibliotekerne/biblioteksudvikling /projekter/projekt-leselyst>

3.4.12 Information literacy

The public library must help its customers develop information literacy, defined as those skills by which a person should be able to recognise when information is needed and have the ability to locate, evaluate, and use effectively the needed information. While pupils in school, students in college and professionals working in learning organisations may have access to a professional librarian with expertise to help them develop independence and self-direction in information seeking the vast majority of the population the public library may serve, does not. What they do have, are information needs and rapidly changing technologies. If they are more fortunate they have a reasonably staffed and funded public library to guide them.

The infosphere can overwhelm any information seeker. And so, public librarians, in the 21st century realise they must do more.

- ▶ In Spain, the Ministry of Culture promotes a group of experts to work in the planning process for public libraries to improve the information literacy skills of the population.
  <http://www.alfinred.org/>
- ▶ "Glasgow REAL Learning Centres" which are part of Glasgow Libraries have a new team in place named Learning Support Officers who staff the centres (including learning portfolios, ITC and the employability agenda). The project is the partnership between Glasgow Libraries and the Chamber of Commerce.
- ▶ The library staff of Mpumalanga and, by extension, rural South Africa were trained to enhance information literacy skills so that they *may improve their service delivery and raise the profile of the public library by enskilling library users."*
- ▶ Access to resources on the World Wide Web have benefited public library customers around the world through access to computers and networked information facilitated by the generous provisions of the Bill and Melinda Gates Foundation.
- ▶ Birmingham (UK) Central Library Learning Centre is integrated into a public library providing access to both the physical and electronic library content resources for independent and collaborative lifelong learning.
- ▶ Christchurch (NZ) City Libraries provide access to 3 learning centres. These are 'learning spaces, services and technology that enable carrying out of group learning programmes and activities with a computer focus.
- ▶ In the Wuhan area, a Chinese public library launched reader-oriented training in information knowledge and technology.
- ▶ Libraries across the globe are providing classes regarding Internet safety for children. The Tampa-Hillsborough County Public Library system in the USA uses the NetSmartz Kids programme to teach internet safety.
  < http://www.hcplc.org/hcplc/justkids/adults/internet.html>

> ‣ A network of 25 libraries <http://smartinvesting.ala.org> is now making resources available to more than 8 million customers at libraries in the USA through Smart investing@your library. Many of these libraries use new ways to reach out to their customers, including YouTube, the virtual world of Second Life, and other social networking tools.

3.5   Customer care

The policies and procedures of the library should be based on the needs and convenience of the customers and not for the convenience of the organisation and its staff. Quality services can only be delivered if the library is sensitive to the needs of its customers and shapes its services to meet those needs. Satisfied customers are the best advocates of the library service.

The public library should have a positive policy of customer care. This means ensuring that in all policy planning, design of libraries and of systems, preparation of operational procedures and drafting of information and publicity material, a positive effect on the customer should be a prime objective. The following actions should be elements in a customer care policy.

Staff related:

- the image projected by all libraries must be neutral and objective
- staff should be courteous, friendly, respectful and helpful at all times
- there should be a regular programme of staff training in customer care
- all staff should receive basic awareness training on how to deal with people with disabilities or from ethnic minorities
- staff should have a friendly and informative telephone manner
- jargon should be avoided in all forms of communication, verbal and written
- all printed information about services should be available in appropriate alternative formats, e.g., large print, tape, CDs, digital formats; they should also be available in alternative languages
- methods of communication with the customers must be provided, e.g., billboards, bulletins, website
- customers should receive a response in the shortest possible time; letters and other forms of communication should be answered promptly and courteously.

Services and facilities:

- library services should be properly planned, adequately prepared and reliable
- the design of the library should be as convenient and inviting as possible
- opening hours should be convenient for the majority of the customers
- library catalogues and websites should be available online so that the customer can access services from home and outside opening hours
- there should be efficient renewal and reservation services including remote access services such as 24 hour telephone or online access
- services should be delivered beyond the library building when customers' needs require it
- equipment should be provided to make library use convenient, e.g., drop-in boxes for returning materials out of hours, self-service issue and return equipment in the library, answering machines, email and voice mail for communicating with the library out of hours
- good quality electronic equipment should be provided in the library including special equipment for the visually and hearing impaired.

3.5.1   Customer participation

Customers should be involved in service development:

- by asking them through surveys what services they use and require
- by analysing and responding to customers' complaints
- by monitoring customers' reactions to services and new initiatives
- by ensuring the input received from customers is considered in the development of policy and procedures
- by providing feedback to customers about the effects of their input on service development
- by providing suggestion boxes and a complaints and commendations procedure
- by conducting Friends' and library customer focus groups
- by gathering information from potential customer groups not using the library

3.6   Customer education

The public library should help its customers develop skills that will enable them to make the most effective use of the library's resources and services. Library staff must act as information navigators to help customers of all ages to make the most effective use of information and communications technology, and programmes of customer education should be developed. As new technologies become more commonly available, the role of the public library both in providing access to these technologies and in helping people learn how to make best use of them is of vital importance.

Guided tours of the library should take place regularly to introduce people to the library building and services and how to use its tools, for example, catalogues and technical equipment. These guided tours have to be carefully planned according to the needs of those taking part. Tours for groups should be organised in co-operation with the institution from which they come.

> ▸ Public libraries in Singapore provide orientation programmes for new and existing customers. Tours of the library are also organised for classes from schools and kindergartens. Information literacy programmes are provided at different levels to assist customers in their search for information.
> ▸ Ten libraries in New Jersey, USA, were given grants to create computer training centres. Grants supported the purchase of PCs and the presentation of computer training courses on a variety of topics.
> ▸ Danish public libraries are active co-players in national programmes which strive to improve citizens' information technology (IT) skills. This is a requirement in the Danish Library Act and supported by two partnership agreements with the National IT and Telecom Agency.
> <http://splq.info/issues/vol42_3/05.htm>

3.7   Co-operation and resource sharing

Overall service to the community is enhanced when libraries develop links for exchanging information, ideas, services and expertise. Such co-operation results in less duplication of service, a combining of resources for maximum effect, and an overall improvement in community services. In addition, individual community members may in some cases be of great assistance in helping the library to carry out special tasks or projects.

The library should facilitate access to other libraries' online catalogues through its own online catalogue/OPAC through links to trusted sites, e.g., regional library systems and the national library website.

▸ Litteratursiden.dk (translated: The Literature site) is a Danish libraries' website which informs the public of new and classic voices from the world of literature, and recommends good books to read. The project is produced and financed by "Foreningen Litteratursiden." <http://www.litteratursiden.dk/>

3.7.1   Formal links

The library should establish formal links with other organisations in the local community, for example, schools, cultural institutions such as museums, galleries and archives, literacy programmes, chambers of commerce or boards of trade. The links should be used to co-ordinate the resources and efforts of each partner and thereby jointly improve services to the community.

3.7.2   Relations with schools

One of the most important institutional relationships for a public library is that with the local schools and the education system in the service area. Types of linkages and/or forms of co-operation include:

- sharing resources
- sharing staff training
- jointly arranged authors' visits
- co-operative collection development
- co-operative programming
- co-ordination of electronic services and networks
- co-operation in the development of learning tools
- class visits to the public library
- joint reading and literacy promotion
- programme of web-awareness for children
- sharing of telecommunications and network infrastructures.

(See *IFLA/UNESCO School Library Manifesto*)

3.7.3   Resource sharing

Each library collection is in some degree unique. No collection can contain all the materials that the members of its public require. Libraries, therefore, can greatly enhance services to their users by providing them with access to the collections of other libraries. Libraries can participate in resource-sharing schemes at any level, local, regional, national and international.

The library should also make its collection available for loan to other libraries through participation in a network, for example, in a union catalogue or in a local network of information providers, such as schools, colleges and universities.

3.7.4   Bibliographic records

The library should classify and catalogue its resources according to accepted international or national bibliographic standards. This facilitates their inclusion in wider networks.

3.7.5   Borrowing from other libraries

In order to meet the information needs of customers the library should borrow materials from other libraries both within the same organisation and beyond. The library should establish interlending policies, which address such issues as:

- lending materials to other public libraries
- the type of materials it is prepared to lend or not to lend
- the length of time for which materials will be lent
- when it will request materials from other libraries
- methods of shipment
- how the costs of the service will be met
- action to be taken if materials are lost or damaged.

3.8   Electronic networks

Public libraries are instruments of equal opportunity and must provide a safety-net against alienation and social exclusion from technological advance by becoming the electronic doorway to information in the digital age. They should enable all citizens to have access to the information that will enable them to manage their lives at the local level, to acquire essential information about the democratic process and to participate positively in an increasingly global society.

The library should provide access to the resources of the library and to those of other libraries and information services through the creation and maintenance of and participation in effective electronic networks at all levels from local to international. This can include participation in community networks, programmes to develop technologically advanced communities and electronic networks linking two or more agencies. They should also be part of national information policies.

- ▶ A virtual public library has been introduced in Denmark. It is now possible to gain access to the catalogues of all public libraries plus the larger research and special libraries. People can order an item from anywhere in the country and collect it at their local library. <http://www.bibliotek.dk>
- ▶ In the UK, many libraries participate in the Enquire service, an electronic reference service which is online 24 hours a day, 365 days of the year with the assistance of librarians internationally. Requests for information are sent online and automatically re-routed to the service. The library then responds directly to the enquirer.
- ▶ Net libraries of Denmark, provides an overview of a number of services directed towards library customers looking for knowledge and information on the internet. <http://bibliotek.dk/netbib.php>
- ▶ The main objective of the project "Establishment and development of all-Russia Virtual Reference Service of Public Libraries" is to optimize the systems of reference and information services for customers of public libraries within the emerging information society with the goal of facilitating socio-political and economic change. <http://www.library.ru/help/>

3.8.1 Customer access

The library should provide free public access to the Internet/World Wide Web to enable all citizens, regardless of economic means, to have access to information available in electronic form. It should have at least one public-access workstation with Internet access and a printer that is not shared with staff.

3.8.2   Remote access

The library should exploit ITC to enable the public to gain access to as many of its electronic resources and services as possible from their home, school or workplace. If possible they should be made accessible 24 hours a day, seven days a week. Making library services available on the Internet increases their accessibility to the public, and to other libraries, and improves the quality of the service.

▸ DelAWARE, developed by Delaware State Library, USA, gives all Delaware citizens access to library information services and the Internet, regardless of geographic location or economic circumstances. It provides a variety of statewide online products and services, state government information, a subject guide to selected Internet sites and links to all types of Delaware libraries.
<http://www.lib.de.us>

▸ Via netmusik.dk, Danish libraries offer access to over 2 million songs and pieces of music, with continuous additions. The music is downloaded directly to the user's PC as a loan, for free. Most Danish public libraries are connected to Netmusik. dk.
<http://netmusik.shop2download.com/cgi-bin/WebObjects/ TShop.woa/wa/default>

▸ Netlydbog.dk (translated: NetAudiobook.dk) is the promotion of audio books online via the Internet in Denmark, in response to the growing demand for digital content on the Internet.
<http://www.netlydbog.dk/>

3.8.3   Staff access

Library staff should have access to the Internet/World Wide Web to enable them to provide better reference and readers' advisory service to customers. Staff should have regular training in using the Internet.

3.8.4   Information navigator

The public library's role is becoming one of mediator, of being the public's electronic doorway to digital information and of helping citizens cross the 'digital divide' to a better future. The librarian's role is increasingly one of 'information navigator' ensuring that the customer gets accurate and reliable information.

3.9   Access to services

Physical accessibility is one of the major keys to the successful delivery of public library services. Services of high quality are of no value to those who are unable to access them. Access to services should be structured in a way that maximises convenience to customers and potential customers.

3.9.1   Location of service outlets

Public library service outlets should be located for the maximum use and convenience of people in the community. Libraries should be near the centre of transport networks and close to areas of community activity, for example, shops, commercial centres, and cultural centres. Where appropriate the public library may share buildings with other services such as arts centres, museums, art galleries, community centres and sports facilities. This can help to attract customers and achieve capital and operational economies.

The outlet should be highly visible and easily reached by foot, public transport, where available, or by private vehicle and in this instance provide convenient parking. In well-developed urban and suburban areas a public library should be available within a journey by private vehicle of about 15 minutes.

Issues of equity of access should be addressed when possible through strategic location of the outlet to reach potential customer groups who may lack any other information access than the public library or knowledge of its services. Outreach delivery may be a part of the solution (see sections 1.10 and 3.4.10).

> ▸ In Singapore, libraries are located in the town centres of government housing. Childrens' libraries are located on the ground floor of apartment blocks and are within five minutes' walk of most children in the neighbourhood.

3.9.2   Opening hours

In order to provide the best possible access to library service, the library must be open at times of maximum convenience to those who live, work and study in the community. This access may extend into 24 hour maintenance of telephone or web access of select services.

3.10   Library buildings

In general when planning a library, the librarian and governing body should consider the following elements:

- the function of the library
- the size of the library
- designated spaces
- design features
- access for the physically handicapped
- signage
- the ambience of the library
- electronic and audiovisual equipment
- safety
- parking.

They should also ensure that the design incorporates flexibility in every aspect including furnishings to accommodate rapidly changing technology and demands for library services.

3.10.1 The function of the library

The library should have adequate space to implement the full range of library services that are consistent with the library's strategic plan and that meet local, area or national standards/guidelines. Libraries in England are asked to meet criteria to assure they meet their obliglations to the community served.
<http://www.culture.gov.uk/Reference_library/Publications/archive _2007/library_standards.htm>

Some of these criteria include:

- proximity of libraries to their customers
- opening hours
- access to the Internet and other items purchased new each year
- number of books and other items purchased new each year

3.10.2 The size of the library

The amount of floor-space required by a public library depends on such factors as the unique needs of the individual community, the functions of the library, the level of resources available, the size of the collection, the space available and the proximity of other libraries. Because these elements will vary significantly from country to country and between different building projects it is not possible to propose a universal standard on the space required for a public library. However local standards have been developed and examples from Ontario, Canada and Barcelona, Spain and Queensland, Australia are included in the appendices, and may be of use in the planning process.

3.10.3 Designated spaces

The library should include space for services to adults, children (including babies and toddlers) and young adults and for family use. It should aim to provide a range of materials to meet the needs of all groups and individuals in the community (see Chapter 4 'Collection development').

The range of functions provided and the space available for each will depend on the size of the library. In planning a new library the following should be considered for inclusion:

- the library collection, including, books, periodicals, special collections, sound recordings, film, and other non-print and digital resources
- reader seating space for adults, children and young adults to use for leisure reading, serious study, group work and one–one tutoring; quiet rooms should be provided
- outreach services: space should be provided to house special collections and preparation areas for outreach services, e.g., mobile library deposit areas.
- staff facilities, including work space (including desks or PC workstations), rest space for eating and relaxing during breaks and meeting rooms where staff can meet with colleagues and supervisors in private
- meeting room space for large and small community groups, which should have separate access to the washrooms and to the exterior to enable meetings to be held while the library is closed
- technology including public access workstations, printers, CD-DVD drives, printers, copiers, scanners, webcams, microfilm/fiche readers

- special equipment, including atlas cases, newspaper racks, self-service book circulation, dictionary stands, wall-mounted display racks, display stands, filing cabinets, map cases etc.
- sufficient space for ease of circulation by both public and staff; this can be 15%–20% of public areas and 20%–25% in staff areas, and allow for at least the minimum access requirements for wheelchair customers
- in larger libraries a café area for the public is a desirable facility or vending machines in smaller libraries
- space must be allowed for the mechanical services of the library, e.g., elevators, heating, ventilation, maintenance, storage of cleaning materials, etc.

3.10.4 Design features

The library should guarantee easy access for all customers and in particular persons with physical and sensory disabilities. The following features should be included in the planning of a new library:

- the exterior of the library should be well lit and identified with signs clearly visible from the street
- the entrance of the library should be clearly visible and located on that part of the building that most users approach.
- the library should focus on eliminating barriers to use
- there should be no design features that limit the ability of an individual or groups to use any part of the library
- care should be taken to avoid steps as much as possible in both interior and exterior design and alternative access provided where use cannot be avoided in the design.
- lighting levels should comply with those stated in international or national standards
- libraries that occupy two or more floors should provide elevators that are close to the library entrance and that easily accommodate wheelchairs and child strollers
- the library should provide facilities for the return of library materials when the library is closed; after-hours deposit boxes should be both theft and waterproof
- a library should undertake an 'accessibility' audit on a regular basis to confirm that there are no barriers to easy use
- local, national or international standards on making public buildings accessible to the disabled should be followed, wherever possible.

3.10.5 Accessible shelving

Materials should be displayed on open shelves and arranged at a height within easy reach for customers and steps and mobile seats provided for any people not able to reach or bend to the levels of the high and low shelves. All shelving should be adjustable and preferably on lockable wheels so that it can easily be moved. The furniture in the children's section should be appropriately sized. Shelves should be of accessible height and width for persons with disabilities.

3.10.6 Signage

The library's exterior signs not only identify the particular function of the building but are also the library's most basic form of publicity. Signs should therefore be carefully planned to communicate an appropriate image of the library. Internal areas of the library and parts of the collection should be clearly identified by signs of a professional standard so that customers can easily find them, for example, the library catalogue, magazines, reference services, the children's area, washrooms, Internet stations, copy machines etc. Signs should also be posted in Braille where necessary. Where appropriate, signs should be provided in languages used by ethnic groups in the community. A sign displaying the opening hours of the library should be clearly visible from outside the library. Talking kiosks, web or audio guides should also be considered to help all customers find their way in the library. Directional signs should be erected in nearby streets and town centres to guide the public to the library and referral from all relevant local web sites assured.

3.10.7 The ambience of the library

The library should provide a physical setting for the library service that is inviting to the public and that provides:

- adequate space to store and display the library collection
- adequate, comfortable and attractive space for the public to make proper and convenient use of the library's services
- adequate quiet space for study and reading
- meeting spaces for groups of various sizes
- sufficient space for the library staff to carry out their duties in an efficient and comfortable setting
- toys and play facilities might be provided in children's areas

- young adult sections could include facilties for computer gaming, "chill out" zones with comfortable seating, and TV or plasma screens
- adequate space and flexibility for the future.

The climate of the library should be maintained at a comfortable temperature, using efficient heating and air conditioning. Humidity control helps to protect the stock as well as increasing the comfort of the library.

Larger libraries may include a café (and smaller libraries vending machines) open either throughout the opening hours of the library or for special occasions. Such facilities are sometimes contracted out to a commercial provider.

▸ In the UK "Ideas Stores" introduced in Tower Hamlets Library Service, London, include cafes as a part of the new interpretation of library service.
<http://www.ideastore.co.uk/>
▸ In Singapore, the concept of 'lifestyle' libraries is being introduced. These include cafés, music listening-posts, and a virtual community for students. All libraries are open seven days a week.

3.10.8 Electronic and audiovisual equipment

A major function of the public library is to bridge the gap between the information rich and the information poor. This includes providing access to the necessary electronic, computer and audiovisual equipment such as personal computers with Internet access, public access catalogues, microform readers, audio and MP3 players, tape recorders, slide projectors and equipment for the visually and physically handicapped. Wireless (wi-fi) access is advisable throughout the library as well as access to electrical outlets for use of personal computers. Wiring should be up-to-date and easily accessible for alterations at a later date. It should also be inspected regularly.

3.10.9 Safety

Every effort should be made to ensure that the library is safe for the public and the staff. Smoke and fire alarms should be provided and security protection for staff and resources. The location of fire extinguishers and emergency exits should be clearly marked. Staff should be trained in first aid and first aid supplies be made readily available. Evacuation drills should be carried out regularly. The library manager in co-operation with the emergency services should prepare a disaster plan to be put into action in the event of a serious incident, for example fire.

3.10.10 Parking

Where customers travel to the library in private vehicles there should be sufficient safe and well lit parking either at or close to the library with appropriately identified spaces for persons with disabilities. If bicycles are a common mode of transport, secure cycle racks should be provided outside the library.

Resources

Bill & Melinda Gates Foundation (2004). *Toward Equality of Access: The Role of Public Libraries in Addressing the Digital Divide.* Seattle: The Foundation. Available at (http://www.imls.gov/pdf/Equality.pdf)

Cylke, F., Byrne, W., Fiddler, H., Zharkov, S.S., and IFLA Section of Libraries for the Blind, Standards Development Committee. (1983). *Approved recommendations on working out national standards of library services for the blind,* available (http://www.nplg.gov.ge/dlibrary/collect/0001/000561/IFLA.pdf)
Note: now called 'Section of Libraries Serving Persons with Print Disabilities' see Kavanaugh reference in this resource list.

Day, J.M., and IFLA Section for Libraries Serving Disadvantaged Persons. (2000). *Guidelines for library services to deaf people,* 2nd ed., Professional report #62. The Hague: IFLA.

de Jager, K., Nassimbeni, M. (2007). *Information Literacy in Practice: engaging public library workers in rural South Africa.* IFLA Journal, Vol. 33, No. 4, 313-322.

EBSCO Industries, Inc. (n.d.). EBSCO Publishing customer success center. (http://www.ebscohost.com/customerSuccess/default.php accessed 1/01/2010).

Fasick, A.. (2008). *Managing children's services in the public library.* Westport, CT: Libraries Unlimited.

IFLA. (n.d.) The IFLA/UNESCO Multicultural Library Manifesto. (http://www.ifla.org/en/publications/the-iflaunesco-multicultural-library-manifesto accessed 1/01/2010).

IFLA Children's and Young Adults Section. (2007). *The Guidelines for Library Services to Babies and Toddlers*. The Hague: IFLA.
(http://archive.ifla.org/VII/d3/pub/Profrep100.pdf accessed 1/01/2010).

IFLA Libraries for Children and Young Adults Section. (2003). *Guidelines for Children's Libraries Services*. The Hague: IFLA.
(http://www.ifla.org/en/publications/guidelines-for-childrens-library-services accessed 1/01/2010).

IFLA Section for Public Libraries. (2003). *The Role of Libraries in Lifelong Learning. Final report of the IFLA project under the Section of Public Libraries*
(http://www.ifla.org/en/publications/the-role-of-libraries-in-lifelong-learning accessed 1/01/2010).

IFLA Public Libraries Section. (2008). Meeting User Needs: A checklist for best practice produced by section 8 – public libraries section of IFLA.
(http://www.ifla.org/VII/s8/proj/Mtg_UN-Checklist.pdf accessed 1/01/2010).

IFLA Section for Library Services to Multicultural Populations. (2009). *Multicultural communities: guidelines for library services*, 3rd ed. The Hague: IFLA.
(http://www.ifla.org/en/publications/multicultural-communities-guidelines-for-library-services-3rd-edition accessed 1/01/2010).

IFLA Section of School Libraries and Resource Centers. (2002). The IFLA/UNESCO School Library Guidelines 2002.
(http://www.ifla.org/en/publications/the-iflaunesco-school-library-guidelines-2002
accessed 1/01/2010).

Kavanaugh, R., Sköld, B.C., and IFLA Section of Libraries Serving Persons with Print Disabilities. (2005). *Libraries for the blind in the information age : Guidelines for development*. The Hague: IFLA.
(http://www.ifla.org/en/publications/ifla-professional-reports-86 accessed 1/01/2010).

Lau, J. (2008). *Information literacy: International perspectives*. Munich: K.G. Saur
(http://archive.ifla.org/V/pr/saur131.htm accessed 1/01/2010).

Li, J. (2002). The Public Library and citizens' information literacy education in China: a case study of Wuhan area, China. IFLA Conference Proceedings, 1-8. Retrieved from Library, Information Science & Technology Abstracts database

Lesk, M. (2005). *Understanding digital libraries*. Amsterdam: Elsevier.

McMenemy, D. and Poulter, A. (2005). *Delivering digital services: A handbook for public libraries and learning centres*. London: Facet.

Melling, M., and Little, J. (2002). *Building a successful customer-service culture: A guide for library and information managers*. London: Facet.

Muller, P., Chew, I., and IFLA Section of Libraries for Children and Young Adults. (2008). *Guidelines for Library Services for Young Adults* The Hague: IFLA.

(http://www.ifla.org/en/publications/revised-guidelines-for-library-services-for-young-adults
accessed 1/01/2010).

Lehmann, V., Locke, J., and IFLA Section for Libraries Serving Disadvantaged Persons. (2005). *Guidelines for library services to prisoners,* 3rd ed. Professional report #34. The Hague: IFLA.
(http://archive.ifla.org/VII/s9/nd1/iflapr-92.pdf accessed 1/01/2010).

Mayo, D. (2005). *Technology for results: Developing service-based plans.* PLA results series. Chicago: American Library Association.

Nielsen, G. S., Irvall, B., and IFLA Section of Libraries for Disadvantaged Persons. (2001). *Guidelines for library services to persons with dyslexia.* The Hague: IFLA.
(http://www.ifla.org/VIIs9/nd1/iflapr-70e.pdf accessed 1/01/2010).

Panella, N.M., and IFLA Section for Libraries Serving Disadvantaged Persons. (2000). *Guidelines for libraries serving hospital patients and the elderly and disabled in long-term care facilities.* Professional report #61. The Hague: IFLA.
(http://archive.ifla.org/VII/s9/nd1/iflapr-61e.pdf
accessed 1/01/2010).

Public Agenda Foundation. (2006). *Long Overdue A Fresh Look at Public Attitudes About Libraries in the 21st Century.* New York: Public Agenda.
(http://www.publicagenda.org/files/pdf/Long_Overdue.pdf
accessed 1/01/2010)

Reading Agency. (n.d.). The Reading Agency. (http://www.readingagency.org.uk/
accessed 1/01/2010).

Ross, C., McKechnie, L., and Rothbauer, P. (2006). *Reading matters: What the research reveals about reading, libraries and community.* Westport, CT: Libraries Unlimited.

Syracuse University College of Law. (n.d.). International and comparative disability law web resources.
(http://www.law.syr.edu/lawlibrary/electronic/humanrights.aspx
accessed 1/01/2010)

UNESCO. (2006). *UNESCO Launches a Community Information Literacy Project at the Tunapuna Public Library* (2007)
(http://portal.unesco.org/en/ev.php-
URL_ID=36505&URL_DO=DO_TOPIC&URL_SECTION=201.html)

Webster, K., and Biggs, B. (2005). *Library services to indigenous populations: Viewpoints & resources.* Chicago: Office for Literacy and Outreach Services, American Library Association.

Weibel, M. (2007). *Adult learners welcome here: A handbook for librarians and literacy teachers.* New York: Neal-Schuman Publishers.

4

Collection development

'Specific services and materials must be provided for those users who cannot, for whatever reason, use the regular services and materials, for example linguistic minorities, people with disabilities or people in hospital or prison.

All age groups must find material relevant to their needs.

Collections and services have to include all types of appropriate media and modern technologies as well as traditional materials. High quality and relevance to local needs and conditions are fundamental. Material must reflect current trends and the evolution of society, as well as the memory of human endeavour and imagination.

Collections and services should not be subject to any form of ideological, political or religious censorship, nor commercial pressures.'

(IFLA/UNESCO Public Library Manifesto, 1994)

4.1   Introduction

The public library should provide equality of access to a range of resources that meets the needs of its customers for education, information, leisure and personal development. The library should provide access to the heritage of its society and develop diverse cultural resources and experiences. Constant interaction and consultation with the local community will help to ensure this objective is achieved.

4.2   Collection management policy

Each public library system requires a written collection management policy, endorsed by the governing body of the library service. The aim of the policy should be to ensure a consistent approach to the maintenance and development of the library collections and access to resources.

It is imperative that collections continue to be developed on an on-going basis to ensure that people have a constant choice of new materials and to meet the demands of new services and of changing levels of use. In light of today's technological advances, the policy must reflect not only a library's own collections but also strategies for accessing information available throughout the world.

The policy should be based upon library standards developed by professional staff related to the needs and interests of local people, and reflecting the diversity of society. The policy should define the purpose, scope and content of the collection, as well as access to external resources.

▶ For some libraries in the Russian Federation, a council of readers helps to determine the acquisition policy.

4.2.1   Content of the policy

The policy may proceed from statements of universal applicability that are relevant to all library services, through more general statements that are relevant to particular countries, or regions, to statements that are specific to particular library services and could include the following elements.

Universal

- Article XIX of the Declaration of Human Rights
- IFLA statement on freedom of access to information
  <http://www.ifla.org/en/publications/ifla-statement-on-libraries-and-intellectual-freedom>
- statements on intellectual freedom, free access to library collections
  <http://www.ifla.org/en/publications/intellectual-freedom-statements-by- others>
- freedom of information
  <http://www.ala.org/ala/issuesadvocacy/intfreedom/librarybill/index.cfm>
- consideration of the Universal Copyright Convention
  <http://archive.ifla.org/documents/infopol/copyright/ucc.txt>
- *IFLA/UNESCO Public Library Manifesto.*
  <http://archive.ifla.org/VII/s8/unesco/eng.htm>

General

- purpose of the collection management policy and its relation to the corporate plan of the library service
- long and short term objectives
- access strategies
- history of the collection and/or library service
- identification of relevant legislation.

Specific

- analysis of community needs
- priorities of the library service
- parameters of the collection, including special collections and collections for special needs, such as multicultural material, literacy and resources for people with disabilities
- selection and discard principles and methods
- budget allocation
- responsibility within the organisation for collection development, selection and discard
- access to electronic resources including online access to periodicals, databases and other information sources
- the role of the library as an electronic gateway to information
- guidelines for identifying and adding free Internet resources
- co-operative relationships with other libraries and organisations
- preservation and conservation policies
- auditing requirements: accessioning, recording, control, discard, sale or disposal
- financial accountability
- donations policy
- complaints procedures and materials challenges
- a resource management plan assessing the current and future needs of the collections
- review and assessment of the policy.

This is not an exhaustive list but an indication of some of the issues that may be included.

4.3   Range of resources

The public library should provide a wide range of materials in a variety of formats and in sufficient quantity to meet the needs and interests of the community. The culture of the local community and society must be reflected in the resource collection. Public libraries must keep abreast of new formats and new methods of accessing information. All information should be as readily available as possible, irrespective of format. The development of local information sources and resources is vital.

▸ The Badalona Can Casacuberta Library customers can follow and learn more about the library on a variety of social networks.
  <http://cancasacuberta.blogspot.com/2007/09/serveis-on-line.html>

▸ Internet Public Library http://www.ipl.org/ ipl2 is a public service organisation and a learning/teaching environment. To date, thousands of students and volunteer library and information science professionals have been involved in answering reference questions for the *Ask an ipl2 Librarian* service and in designing, building, creating and maintaining the ipl2's collections. It is through the efforts of these students and volunteers that the ipl2 continues to thrive to this day.

▸ Many USA libraries, like the Tarrant County library in Texas, are adding resources that customers can access over the Internet. Tarrant County library cards provide online access to practice college entrance and licensing exams; talking, animated storybooks via the library website; and downloadable audio books.

4.3.1   Collections

The following categories of library materials many of which are increasingly electronic, may be represented in a typical public library, although this list is not exhaustive:

- fiction and non-fiction for adults, young adults and children
- reference works
- access to databases
- periodicals
- local, regional and national newspapers
- community information
- government information, including information by and about local administrations
- business information
- local history resources

- genealogical resources
- resources in the primary language of the community
- resources in alternative languages in the community
- resources in other languages
- music scores
- computer games
- toys
- games and puzzles
- study materials.

4.3.2   Formats

The following formats may be included in a public library collection although this list is not exhaustive and new formats are continually appearing:

- books, hard and soft covers and e-books
- pamphlets and ephemera
- newspapers and periodicals including cuttings files, online and print
- digital information through the Internet
- online databases
- software programmes
- microforms
- tapes and compact discs (CDs) including dowloadable format
- digital versatile discs (DVDs) including downloadable format
- videocassettes
- large print materials
- braille materials
- audio books and recordings, including dowloadable format
- MP3s
- art and posters.

4.3.3   Selection Aids

Given the wide range of resources available, public libraries use selection aids to identify well-received or authoritative materials in all formats. Common selection aids include but are not limited to the following:

- bibliographies
- lists of award-winners, recommended items, or core collection suggestions

- directories listing periodical publications in a particular subject area
- reviews
- publishers' catalogues, flyers, and announcements
- book fairs.

4.4   Collection development

Collections complement services and should not be seen as an end in themselves, unless their specified primary purpose is the preservation and conservation of resources for future generations.

Large collections are not synonymous with good collections, particularly in the new digital world. The relevance of the collection to the needs of the local community is more important than the size of the collection.

Collection size is determined by many factors, including space, financial resources, catchment population of the library, proximity to other libraries, regional role of the collections, and access to electronic resources, assessment of local needs, acquisition and discard rates, and policy of stock exchanges with other libraries.

4.4.1   Criteria for collections

The main criteria for collections should be:

- a range of resources that caters to all members of the community
- resources in formats that enable all members of the community to make use of the library service
- inflow of new titles
- inflow of new books and other materials
- turnover of stock
- a wide range of fiction categories and of non-fiction subject coverage
- provision of non-print resources
- access to external resources such as libraries of other institutions, electronic resources, local societies, government departments or the community's knowledge of oral cultures
- discard of old, worn and outdated books, non-print resources and information sources.

Many libraries post collection development policies on the web. When seeking a model to emulate, select a library of comparable service population, in size and customer characteristics.

▸ Cambridge University Library in the United Kingdom (UK) published collection development policies for a combined library serving the public and a university.
<http://www.lib.cam.ac.uk/>
▸ Pasadena, CA
<http://ww2.cityofpasadena.net/LIBRARY/collection.asp>
and Newark, NJ
<http://www.npl.org/Pages/AboutLibrary/colldevpol06.html>
in the USA, offer mid to large size urban collection development models.

4.5   Collection maintenance principles

Public libraries of any size will contain materials in a variety of formats. Collection maintenance applies equally to all materials whatever their format. Materials on open access should be in good physical condition and contain current information. A smaller, high quality stock will result in more usage than a large stock with a high proportion of old, worn and outdated materials, in which newer titles can be lost among mediocre stock. Using outdated reference material can result in the customer being given inaccurate information.

Materials in digital formats complement print collections and will replace them in certain areas. Reference works and periodicals in electronic databases and on the web may be more viable and may be preferred alternatives to printed formats.

4.5.1   Acquisition and deselection

The library collection is a dynamic resource. It requires a constant inflow of new material and outflow of old material to ensure that it remains relevant to the community and at an acceptable level of accuracy. The size and quality of the stock should reflect the needs of the community.

Acquisition rates are more significant than collection size. The acquisition rate is often determined largely by the size of the resource budget or the effectiveness of the negotiated contract with suppliers. However, it can also be affected by other factors, for example:

• the availability of materials published in local languages
• the population served
• the level of use

- the multicultural and linguistic diversity
- age distribution of the population
- special needs such as people with disabilities or older persons
- access to online information.

Deselection is an equally important part of collection maintenance. Criteria for deselection include the following:

- Materials receiving little or no use
- Materials duplicated elsewhere in the collection
- Worn-out, damaged materials
- Obsolete or irrelevant materials.

Discarded materials may be disposed of or sold. Deselecting materials frees up space for new materials, and helps to maintain the overall quality of the collection.

4.5.2   Reserve stocks

It may be necessary to maintain a collection of older and lesser-used materials on shelves not directly accessible to the public. This should only contain materials that have a current or future use and that cannot be replaced or found in any other format. This may include special subject collections that are used on a regular, if limited, basis and out-of-print fiction. Materials that contain outdated information or are in poor condition and can be replaced, should be discarded and not held in a reserve stock. It is efficient to maintain a co-operative reserve with other libraries. The maintenance of a reserve stock should be a regular and on-going activity. The availability of a wide range of information on the Internet and electronic resources reduces the need for public libraries to keep extensive reserve stocks.

4.5.3   Interlending

No library or library service can be self-sufficient in stock, and an efficient and effective interlibrary loan system should be an essential part of every public library service. Within a library service with several outlets a regular programme of exchange of stock between libraries makes maximum use of the stock and provides customers with a greater variety of titles from which to choose.

Many libraries with multiple outlets (sometimes called branches) are now "floating" their collections. Circulating materials no longer belong to one location but remain at the library to which they are returned by the customer thus refreshing the collection, saving time in transit to a "home" library and reducing materials handling.

4.6   Standards for collections

The following proposed standards relate to collection size. Local and financial circumstances could lead to variations in these proposed standards. Where resources are severely limited these may be regarded as target figures and medium and long-term strategies should be developed to work towards achieving these standards in the future.

▸ As a general guide an established collection should be between 2 to 3 items per capita. With large service populations (100 000 and over), this number may increase.
○ Queensland, Australia's public library standards recommend 3 items per capita for populations under 50 000, and 2-3 items for populations over 50 000.
○ In the United States, standards for Florida public libraries recommend a minimum of 3 items per capita for populations under 25 000, and 2 items per capita for populations greater than 25 000.
▸ The minimum stock level for the smallest service point should not be less than 2500 items.
○ Queensland, Australia's standards recommend a minimum collection size of 2500, regardless of population.
○ Standards for Florida public libraries recommend a minimum of 10 000 items.

In the smallest collections, materials for children, adult fiction and adult non-fiction may be provided in equal proportions. In larger collections, the percentage of non-fiction titles will tend to increase. These ratios can vary according to the needs of the local community and the role of the public library. Relevant collections to serve the needs of young adults should be developed (see *IFLA's Guidelines for Library Services for Young Adults*). Where the library has a strong educational role this is likely to be reflected in the composition of the stock.

Where reliable population figures are not available alternative methods of developing standards are needed. The estimated size of the community served, the size of the library, and the number of current and anticipated customers can be used as a basis for developing standards for the size of the collection. Comparisons with a number of existing libraries serving communities of a similar size and make-up can be used to determine a target figure for the size of the collection and the resources needed to maintain it.

4.7   Standards for electronic information facilities

The following standards relate to technology, specifically to computers and Internet access.

> ▸ A standard of one computer access point per 5000 population has been used in Canada.
> ▸ In Queensland, Australia it is recommended that the following be provided:
>   o   for populations up to 200 000 – one public PC per 5000 population.
>   o   for populations over 200 000 – one public PC per 2500 population.
>   o   These standards recommend that at least 75% of the public PCs in each library should have access to the Internet, and all should have access to a printer.
> ▸ In the United States, Florida public library standards recommend a minimum of 1 public PC per 3000 population, all of which should be connected to the Internet.

4.8   Collection development programme for new libraries

An assessment is required of the demographics of the community in the catchment areas of proposed new library developments to determine the initial mix of collections. The development of local and regional standards should be undertaken to take account of variations in the catchment population to be served by the new library. The following recommended standards relate to the stages of collection building for a new library.

4.8.1   Establishment phase

A basic collection should be established in new libraries to serve the needs of the general population within the catchment area. A sufficient range and depth of resources to meet general needs should be the aim at this stage rather than comprehensive coverage. The interlibrary loan system should be at its peak utilisation during this phase to supplement the developing collections. In some countries materials from a national or provincial centre are used to supplement the local stock. Access to both print and digital information sources should be included in this phase of development.

4.8.2 Consolidation phase

The objective under this phase is to achieve growth in the stock size, range and depth. Special conditions of the population are taken into account and collections developed to meet the more in-depth needs of the population served. The book discard factor comes into play and the collection growth rate decreases as discards begin to offset acquisitions.

4.8.3 Steady-state phase

The collections meet the needs of the community in depth, range and quantity. The quality of collections is maintained by acquisition rates matching deselection rates. New formats are accommodated within the collections as they become available, and access is provided to the widest possible range of resources through the use of technology.

4.8.4 Content creation

The service should become a content creator and a preserver of local community resources. Content creation includes publication of information booklets and the development of web content by providing access to information about the library or held by the library in printed formats. The library should also position itself as a guide to content available on the Internet, by highlighting useful websites and other materials that are available online.

▸ Eight public libraries in Vejle, Denmark, co-operate in maintaining a website covering all the cultural events in the region. More than 2000 local organisations are supported on the website to promote their activities. <http://www.netopnu.dk>

4.9   Acquisition and deselection rates

For general stock in an established library service, standard acquisition and deselection rates may be applied. A sample acquisition formula is provided.

Population	per annum	acquisitions per annum
Below 25 000	0.25	250
25 000–50 000	0.225	225
50 000+	0.20	200

The following examples suggest the collection size for communities of different sizes.

Scenario 1

• Established library service serving 100 000 population
• Median stock of 200 000 volumes
• Annual acquisition rate of 20 000 volumes

Scenario 2

• Established library service serving 50 000 population
• Median stock of 100 000 volumes
• Annual acquisition rate of 11 250 volumes

Scenario 3

• Established library service serving 20 000 population
• Median stock of 40 000 volumes
• Annual acquisition rate of 5000 volumes.

▸ Queensland, Australia's public library standards offer acquisition rates based on service population.
  o For populations under 25 000, .3 items per capita per annum.
  o For populations between 25 000 and 100 000, .25 items per capita per annum.
  o For populations over 100 000, .2 items per capita per annum.
▸ In the United States, Florida public libraries standards recommend annually deleting at least 5% of the total number of items available, and adding each year a percentage to achieve overall collection size goal.

4.9.1   Small libraries and mobile libraries

The general acquisition rates would be inadequate to meet the needs of small libraries and mobile libraries where stock numbers are limited. All libraries require a certain minimum stock in order to provide a sufficient range of materials from which customers may make their selection. The acquisition rate of 250 items per 1000 population may not be relevant in the smallest service points, where physical limitations may reduce stock levels below the minimum recommended level of 2500 volumes. In these cases the acquisition rates, renewal rates or exchange rates should be based upon the collection size rather than the population served, and be in the order of 100% or more per annum. An efficient interlibrary loan system is essential in these situations.

4.9.2   Special collections

General acquisition and discard rates may not be relevant to some parts of the collection or to particular special collections or where special circumstances prevail. In these cases the collection policy must reflect the special needs. Particular examples of these exceptions are:

- indigenous resources – the public library has a role in maintaining and promoting collections of resources related to the culture of indigenous people and ensuring access to them
- local history resources – material relating to the history of the locality should be actively collected, preserved and made available
- libraries in communities with a high proportion of particular groups, e.g., children, retired people, young adults, indigenous peoples, ethnic minorities or unemployed people should reflect the needs of these groups in their collections and services
- reference collections – older reference material may need to be retained to provide historical data for research.
- digital collections – unlike print collections, digital collections are not constrained by shelf space. However, digital items should still be removed from the collection if they are no longer useful, current, or appropriate.

4.10   Digital collection management

Digital collections have many criteria in common with traditional collections. They should match the scope of the overall collection, meet demand and levels of use, and be assessed regularly. There are, however, additional considerations for digital materials.

- Access – not all library customers have the technology required to access digital resources. It is important to consider whether access is expanded or diminished by acquiring a digital resource over a print resource.
- Financial and technical issues – if the library maintains digital resources internally, long term cost can exceed that of print items, as it requires time and money to transfer the digital files to new formats periodically as technologies change.
- Legal issues – The public library must be aware of any copyright laws that apply to digital resources, over and above copyright laws affecting print resources. Additionally, censorship and intellectual freedom are issues for public libraries with respect to materials customers access using library-provided computers and Internet access.
- Licensing – Vendors of digital content, like electronic serials, frequently have complex licensing terms that may limit numbers of concurrent users, downloads, off-site access, user privacy, and perpetual access. It is important to understand the terms of each license agreement.

Digital collections are an important part of a public library's collection. Libraries may consider developing a separate collection policy for digital materials to deal with their unique qualities.

Resources

American Library Association. (2003). Negotiating contracts with database vendors. (http://www.ala.org/ala/mgrps/divs/pla/plapublications/platechnotes/negoti ating. pdf
accessed 1/01/2010).

Alabaster, C. (2002). *Developing an outstanding core collection: A guide for libraries.* Chicago: American Library Association.

Cassell, K.A., and IFLA. (2008). *Gifts for the Collections: Guidelines for Libraries.* IFLA professional report #112. The Hague: IFLA.
(http://www.ifla.org/en/publications/ifla-professional-reports-112
accessed 1/01/2010).

Ellis, S., Heaney, M., Meunier, P., and Poll, R. (2009.) "Global Library Statistics."
IFLA Journal. vol. 35(2): pp. 123.
(http://archive.ifla.org/V/iflaj/IFLA-Journal-2-2009.pdf
accessed 1/01/2010).

Evans, G. E.; and Zarnosky, M.R. (2005). *Developing library and information center collections.* Westport, Conn ; London : Libraries Unlimited.

Griffey, J. (2010). *Mobile technologies and libraries.* Neal-Schuman.

Heaney, M. (2009). *Library statistics for the twenty-first century world: Proceedings of the conference held in Montréal on 18-19 August 2008 reporting on the global library statistics project.* Munich: K G Saur.

IFLA. (2002). *The IFLA Internet Manifesto.*
(http://www.ifla.org/publications/the-ifla-internet-manifesto
accessed 1/01/2010).

IFLA. (2001). *Licensing principles.* (http://www.ifla.org/en/publications/licensing-principles accessed 1/01/2010).

IFLA Section on Acquisition and Collection Development. (2001). *Guidelines for a Collection Development Policy Using the Conspectus Model.* The Hague: IFLA.
(http://www.ifla.org/en/publications/guidelines-for-a-collection-development-policy-using-the-conspectus-model
accessed 1/01/2010).

Johnson, P. (2009). *Fundamentals of Collection Development and Management.* Chicago: American Library Association.

Library & Information Association of New Zealand Aotearoa (LIANZA). (2004). *Standards for New Zealand Public Libraries, 2004.* Wellington: N.Z.

Muller, P., Chew, I., and IFLA Section of Libraries for Children and Young Adults. (2008). *Guidelines for Library Services for Young Adults* The Hague: IFLA.
(http://www.ifla.org/en/publications/revised-guidelines-for-library-services-for-young-adults
accessed 1/01/2010).

National Information Standards Organization (NISO). (2008). *SERU: A Shared Electronic Resource Understanding.* NISO RP-7-2008.
(http://www.niso.org/workrooms/seru;
http://www.niso.org/publications/rp/RP-7-2008.pdf
accessed 1/01/2010).

Poll, R. (2009). Bibliography "Impact and outcome of libraries." International Federation of Library Associations and Institutions (IFLA).
(http://www.ifla.org/files/statistics-and-evaluation/publications/bibliography-impact-outcome.pdf accessed 1/01/2010
accessed 1/01/2010).

State Library of New South Wales, Heather Nesbitt Planning, Library Council of New South Wales, and Bligh, Voller, Nield. (2005). *People Places: A Guide for Public Library Buildings in New South Wales.* Sydney: Library Council of New South Wales.
(http://www.sl.nsw.gov.au/services/public_libraries/library_mgt/lib_management_ docs/peopleplaces_2ndedition.pdf accessed 1/01/2010).

State Library of Queensland. (n.d.). Queensland Public Library standards and guidelines.
(http://www.slq.qld.gov.au/info/publib/policy/guidelines
accessed 1/01/2010).

Yale University Library. (n.d.). Liblicense: Licensing digital information: A resource for librarians.
(http://www.library.yale.edu/~llicense/index.shtml
accessed 1/01/2010).

5

Human resources

'The public library has to be organised effectively and professional standards of operation must be maintained.

The librarian is an active liaison between users and resources. Professional and continuing education of the librarian is indispensable to ensure adequate services.'

(IFLA/UNESCO Public Library Manifesto, 1994)

5.1   Introduction

Staff are a vitally important resource in the operation of a library. Staff expenses normally represent a high proportion of a library's budget. In order to provide the best possible service to the community it is necessary to maintain well trained and highly motivated staff to make effective use of the resources of the library and to meet the demands of the community. Staff should be available in sufficient numbers during all hours to carry out these responsibilities.

The management of library staff is itself an important task. All staff should have a clear understanding of the policy of the library service, well-defined duties and responsibilities, properly regulated conditions of employment and salaries that are competitive with other similar jobs.

5.2   The skills of library staff

As the demands on libraries become more diverse, specific skills of staff are required beyond what is found in a general job description. Competencies to attain these skills may be learned through on the job training, continuing education or based upon prior experience. Staff skills traditionally related to the practices and procedures of the organisation, but now and more often relate to technology, customer service and interpersonal skills. The fundamental qualities and skills often required of staff can be defined as:

- the ability to communicate positively with people
- the ability to understand the needs of customers
- the ability to co-operate with individuals and groups in the community
- knowledge and understanding of cultural diversity
- knowledge of the material that forms the library's collection and how to access it
- an understanding of and sympathy with the principles of public service
- the ability to work with others in providing an effective library service
- organisational skills, with the flexibility to identify and implement changes
- teamwork and leadership skills
- imagination, vision and openness to new ideas and practice
- readiness to change methods of working to meet new situations
- knowledge of information and communications technology as these change.

▸ Queensland Standards and Guidelines for Public Libraries
  (see Appendix 6, 2. *Staffing standards*) offers a link
  <http://www.alia.org.au/policies/core.knowledge.html>
  to criteria for staff skills and attributes issued by the Australian Library and Information Association.
▸ WebJunction includes a list of American Library Association (ALA) and US state library organisations' staff competencies within the *Competency Index*.
  <http://www.webjunction.org/competencies>

5.3   Staff categories

The following categories of staff are found in public libraries:

- qualified librarians
- library assistants
- specialist staff
- support staff.

In some countries there is an additional category of library technician, or para-professional, with an intermediate level of qualifications.

Staff in all categories may be appointed on either a full-time or part-time basis. In some countries two or more people share a single post, a practice known as job-sharing. This provides the opportunity to appoint and retain experienced staff that may not be able to work full-time.

5.3.1   Qualified librarians

Qualified librarians are professional staff who have undertaken a course of study in librarianship and information studies to degree or post-graduate level. A librarian designs, plans, organises, implements, manages and evaluates library and information services and systems to meet the needs of the customers in the community. This will include collection development, the organisation and exploitation of resources, the provision of advice and assistance to customers in finding and us-ing information and the development of systems that will facilitate ac-cess to the library's resources. Qualified librarians must know and un-derstand the community and have regular contact with members of the community that they serve. Expertise in specific areas, for example, management, children's materials and services and reference should be encouraged as needed, and when forming the professional team.

The following is a list of some of the duties of the qualified librar-ian. This list is not exhaustive nor is it likely that the qualified librarian will undertake all these activities simultaneously:

Planning and administration:

- analysing the resource and information needs of the community
- formulating and implementing policies for service development
- planning services for the public and participating in their delivery
- developing acquisition policies and systems for library resources
- managing and administering library and information services and systems

Information provision:

- retrieving and presenting information
- answering reference and information enquiries using appropriate material
- assisting customers in the use of library resources and information
- providing readers' advisory services

Marketing:

- developing services to meet the needs of special groups, e.g., children
- promoting library services
- advocating for libraries, services and staff

Information organization:

- creating and maintaining databases to meet the needs of the library and its customers
- designing library and information services and systems to meet the needs of the public
- cataloguing and classification of library materials
- keeping up-to-date with current developments in the information profession and relevant technologies

Evaluation and monitoring:

- evaluating library services and systems and measuring their performance
- selecting, evaluating, managing and training staff

Facility management:

- participation in planning the design and layout of new and refurbished libraries and of mobile libraries

Collection development:

- selecting and purchasing library materials for stock
- developing reading with customers

Customer education:

- providing educational and training opportunities for the community
- developing services to meet the needs of special groups.

5.3.2   Paraprofesional staff

The duties of paraprofessional staff may typically include: supervision of non-professional staff and staff scheduling; routine public and technical service functions; and building and facilities maintenance. They will often be experienced staff who the public will come into contact with most frequently. It is essential, therefore, that they should have a high level of interpersonal and communication skills and receive appropriate training. These positions may offer opportunity for education and career development into professional librarian positions.

5.3.3 Library assistants

Library assistants may most often be employed by larger public libraries to carry out routine and operational library tasks such as circulation activities, shelving, processing library materials, data entry, filing, clerical support and greet and direct customers. They may also assist with children's programming and arts and crafts.

5.3.4 Specialist staff

Larger public libraries may employ specialist staff to carry out specific functions, for example, computer system managers, administrative, financial, facility engineers, training and marketing staff. Specialist staff generally have a qualification in their specialty area rather than in librarianship.

5.3.5 Support staff

Support staff include caretakers, cleaners, drivers and security staff. They carry out important functions, which contribute to the smooth operation of the library service. They should be regarded as an integral part of the library's staff.

5.3.6 The composition of the staff

The composition of the staff should, as far as possible, reflect the make-up of the population it serves. For example, in a community with a significant number of people from a particular ethnic group within the community, the library staff should include members of that group. The same can be said for multiple language groups. Reflecting these diversities within the population demonstrates that the library is a service for everyone and seeks to attract customers from all sections of the public. Libraries should also be in accord with local and national (governance) employment laws.

5.4   Ethical standards

Public library staff have a responsibility to maintain high ethical standards in their dealings with the public, other members of staff and external organisations. All members of the public should be dealt with on an equal basis and every effort must be made to ensure that information provided is as full and accurate as possible. Library staff must not allow their personal attitudes and opinions to determine which members of the public are served and what materials are selected and displayed. The public must have confidence in the impartiality of the library staff if the library is to meet the needs of all members of the community. Library associations in some countries have developed codes of ethics, which can be used as models to introduce similar codes elsewhere. The IFLA/FAIFE website includes details of over 20 codes of ethics for librarians from various countries.

5.5   The duties of library staff

The operation of a library should be a team effort with a close working relationship between all members of staff. It is important, however, that staff are used primarily for tasks related to their skills and qualifications. It is a wasteful use of scarce resources, for example, for qualified librarians to regularly carry out routine circulation functions. For the same reason it is not necessary to have a qualified librarian in every library regardless of size or circulation rate. Small libraries open for limited hours do not require the continuous presence of a qualified librarian. They should however be under the supervision of a member of the qualified staff. All customers should have access to a qualified librarian whether in person, by telephone or online. Staff should have a written agreement at the time of their appointment, which clearly states their duties and responsibilities. These should not be changed without consulting the member of staff involved.

5.6   Staffing levels

The number of staff required in each library service will be affected by a range of factors, for example, the number of library buildings, their size and layout, the number of departments within each building, the level of use, services provided beyond the library and requirements for specialist staff. Where some services are provided or supplemented by a regional or national central agency this will have an impact on the number of staff required at the local level. The level of available resources is also a critical factor.

A method of developing an appropriate staffing level for a library service would be to carry out a process of bench-marking with libraries of comparative size and similar characteristics.

5.7   Education of librarians

Qualified librarians will have undertaken a degree or post-graduate courses at a school of library and information studies. To ensure that they remain in touch with the latest developments, librarians should maintain a process of continuing professional development on a formal and informal basis. It is important that public librarians try to maintain close links with the schools of librarianship (and vice versa) in their country and are fully aware of course content. Whenever possible they should participate in the work of the library and information studies schools, for example, by contributing lectures, assisting in interviewing of prospective students, providing internships and other appropriate forms of co-operation.

5.8   Training

Training is a vital element of the activities of a public library. There must be a planned and continuous programme of training for staff at all levels, which should include both full-time and part-time staff. The rapid developments in information technology make the need for regular training even more essential, and the importance of networking and access to other information sources should be included in training programmes. Specialist and support staff should receive induction training in the functions and purpose of the public library and the context in which it operates.

In budgeting for the implementation of new systems, an element should be included for training. In large library services a post of training or personnel officer should be created to plan and implement the training programme. To ensure funds are available for training a set percentage of the budget should be earmarked for this function.

▸ It is recommended that 0.5%–1% of the total library budget should be earmarked for training purposes.
▸ Training is offered to staff on site and via the web by FL (USA) regional support centers. <http://www.neflin.org/> and <http://www.tblc.org/training/index.php>

This level of funding for training should be maintained at times of budget reductions as the need for a well-trained staff is very important in such circumstances.

5.8.1   Mentoring

An effective and economical method of training is to introduce a system of mentoring. New staff work with a more experienced colleague who provides guidance and training. The mentor should be able to advise the new member of staff about issues relating to their work and employment. A checklist of the training provided by the mentor should be maintained to ensure that it is carried out effectively.

5.8.2   Contacts

In addition to in-service training, staff should be given opportunities to attend short courses in person or via the Internet, and conferences relevant to their ability to carry out their work. They should be encouraged to be active members of the relevant library association, as this creates links with other library staff and provides opportunities for an exchange of ideas and experience. It may also be possible to arrange staff exchanges with staff in other libraries, either in the same country or in a similar library in another country, which can be a valuable experience for all those involved.

5.9   Career development

In order to motivate and retain skilled staff, opportunities for career development should be available at all levels. A scheme of performance review should be in place that provides staff with an evaluation of current performance and guidance in improving and developing their skills. These periodic reviews also present an opportunity to mentor and direct career progression. Post employment (or continuing education) training provided by professional organisations and public libraries is a vital ingredient contributing to career development as well.

5.10   Working conditions

All library staff should have satisfactory working conditions, and the conditions of employment should be clearly stated in the agreement given to the new member of staff when they are employed. Salaries should be at a level appropriate to the level of work being undertaken and competitive with other similar jobs in the community.

5.10.1 Health and safety

The health and safety of staff must be a high priority and policies and procedures put in place to reduce risks. Consideration should be given to:

- good working conditions for staff
- ergonomically designed furniture and equipment
- availability of technical aids for employees with special needs and disabilities
- the drawing up of evacuation plans and their testing on a regular basis
- identified health and safety risks being rectified at the earliest opportunity
- ensuring that all equipment and cabling conforms with recognised safety standards
- the establishment of a staff health and safety committee
- appointment and training of staff as first-aid officers and fire wardens
- provision of safety devices for staff, particularly when staff work at nights or away from the library
- providing advanced driver training for staff who drive library vehicles
- protective clothing when required
- limiting the weight of cartons and loads on book trolleys.

Public libraries are often open for long hours including evenings and weekends. In creating work schedules for staff every effort should be made to ensure that their working hours provide them with adequate time off at appropriate times for social activity. It is vital that good labour relations are maintained and fostered with staff.

5.10.2 Problem customers

In any building freely accessible to the public, staff will occasionally encounter customers who behave in an unpleasant and anti-social manner. Staff should be trained in how to deal with such situations and have internal communication systems which can alert other staff. Full records of such occurrences should be kept. A system should be developed to support library staff who may deal with these situations, involving other staff such as security guards, or government social workers. A strong realtionship with all relevant community agencies is very important – so if staff are in situations which they are not qualified or able to handle, they and the library will have ready backing.

5.11   Volunteers

Where a library uses volunteer help from individuals in the community to assist library staff, a written policy should be in place defining the tasks of these volunteers and their relationship to the library operation and staff. Volunteers should not be used as a substitute for paid staff (see volunteer policies within *Sample policies* in this chapter's resource list).

▸ The Greenfield Public Library, MA (USA) Volunteer Programme is designed to expand and enhance public service to the community. Volunteers generally provide support services to paid staff; work on special projects; or deliver library materials to the homebound. Volunteers are expected to act in accordance with library human resouces policies and to reflect the library's positive customer service attitude.
<http://www.greenfieldpubliclibrary.org/Volunteer.html>

Resources

Cohn, J. & Kelsey, A. (2006). *Staffing the modern library*. New York, NY: Neal-Schuman Publishers, Inc.

Gorman, M. (2003). *The enduring library: technology, tradition, and the quest for balance.* Chicago: American Library Association.

Goodrich, J. (2007). *Human resources for results: The right person for the right job.* Chicago: American Library Association.

Haley, C. K. (2009). Online Workplace Training in Libraries. Information Technology and Libraries.
(http://www.ala.org/ala/mgrps/divs/lita/ital/272008/2701mar/haley_html.cfm accessed 20/11/09)

IFLA. (n.d.) *Professional codes of ethics for librarians.*
(http://www.ifla.org/en/faife/professional-codes-of-ethics-for-librarians)

Jain, P. (2005). "Strategic human resource development in Botswana." *Library Management* (26) 6/7: pp: 336-350.

Jenkins, H. et. al. (2006). *Confronting the Challenges of Participatory Culture: Media Education for the 21ˢᵗ Century.* Newmedialiteracies.org. Chicago, IL.: The MacArthur Foundation.

(http://www.newmedialiteracies.org/files/working/NMLWhitePaper.pdf accessed 15/11/09).

Mid-Huston Library System (n.d.) Trustee resources: *Sample public library policy and development tips.*
(http://midhudson.org/department/member_information/library_policies.htm accessed 3/09/2010)

Moran, B., Ed. (2003) *Training skills for library staff.* Lanham, Md: Rowman & Littlefield Publishing Group, Inc.

Oh, K. & Yunkeum, K. (2005). *Developing a dynamic Korean public library system.*
(http://archive.ifla.org/IV/ifla72/papers/130-Oh_Chang-en.pdf accessed 12/11/09).

Preer, J. (2008). *Library ethics.* Littleton, CO: Libraries Unlimited.

Pugh, L. (2005). *Managing 21st century libraries.* Lanham, Md.: Scarecrow Press.

Rubin, R. (1991). *Human resource management in libraries: theory and practice.* New York, NY: Neal-Schuman Publishers, Inc.

Todaro, J. & Smith, M.L. (2006). *Training library staff and volunteers to provide extraordinary customer service.* New York: Neal-Schuman Publishers.

Online Computer Library Center (OCLC). (n.d.). "Webjunction: Where librarians and library staff connect, create and learn."
(http://www.webjunction.org accessed 1/01/2010).

Whitmell, V. Ed. (2005). *Staff planning in a time of demographic change.* Lanham, Md.: Scarecrow Press.

6

The management of public libraries

'A clear policy must be formulated defining objectives, priorities and services in relation to the local community needs. The public library has to be organised effectively and professional standards of operation must be maintained.'

(IFLA/UNESCO Public Library Manifesto, 1994)

6.1 Introduction

A successful public library is a dynamic organisation working with other institutions and with individuals to provide a range of library and information services to meet the varied and changing needs of the community. To be effective it requires experienced, flexible and well trained managers and staff able to use a range of management techniques. This chapter deals with the key elements of public library management.

6.2 Management skills

Management of a public library involves a number of different skills:

- leadership and motivation
- maintaining effective relationships with governing and funding bodies
- planning and policy development
- building and maintaining networks with other organisations
- budget negotiations and management
- management of library resources
- staff management
- planning and development of library systems
- the management of change
- marketing and promotion

- community liaison and lobbying
- raising funds from alternative funding sources.

6.2.1   Leadership and motivation

The library manager has a vital role in advocating the value of public libraries as an integral part of an international, national and local infrastructure. He/she must promote public libraries to politicians and key stakeholders at all levels in order to ensure they are aware of the importance of public libraries and to attract adequate funding for their maintenance and development. The library manager must ensure that governing authorities are informed of new developments that may impact on public library services and are also made aware that the library's services are key players in providing access to the delivery of new services.

The library manager is responsible for the motivation of staff and bringing energy, vitality and strength into the library service and its staff. The manager also plays a key role in managing the development of physical facilities and ensuring that the most effective use is made of resources, including information technology, to enable the library service to meet the library and information needs of the community.

6.2.2   Relationships with governing and funding bodies

To achieve its goals the public library needs adequate and sustained funding. It is very important that the library manager establishes and maintains a close and positive relationship with the bodies that govern the library service and provide its funding (this is sometimes called advocacy). The library manager as head of the public library service should have direct access to and involvement with the board or committee that is directly responsible for the library service. As well as formal meetings there should be regular informal contacts between the library manager and members of the governing body, and they should be kept well informed about the library service and current and future developments.

6.2.3   Planning and policy development

Planning ensures that:

- the library responds to the needs of the community
- the governing body, management and staff understand what the library is trying to achieve

- community funds are spent in an effective and responsible manner
- continuity of service is maintained regardless of changes of personnel
- the library expands the expectations of the community as new services are developed
- the library is able to respond effectively to change.

The determination of public library goals, short and long term objectives, strategies and performance measurement is necessary to ensure equitable, effective and efficient library service provision with access for all sectors of the community. Strategic and operational plans require formulation, documentation and adoption.

Planning should not take place in isolation but in conjunction with the governing and funding bodies, the library staff and the actual and potential clients served. A strategic plan must be customer-focused and should include the following elements:

- review of achievements
- examination of needs
- vision and mission statements
- identification of priorities and short term goals
- development of strategies for achieving goals
- identification of critical success factors
- budget allocation
- deployment of resources to achieve optimum performance
- measurement and evaluation of input, output and outcome measures for customers
- reassessment of needs and policies.

6.2.4   Operational planning

An operational plan is necessary to ensure that the activities of the library service are focused on achieving the priorities and goals identified in the strategic plan. The plan should reflect the following elements:

- a focus on service to customers
- the implementation of the priorities and goals of the strategic plan
- the formation of operational elements of the agreed strategies
- the development of clearly identified goals with manageable and achievable time frames
- the definition of achievable outputs for the level of inputs
- the participation of library staff who carry out the activities

- the allocation of responsibility to identified staff members for achieving outputs
- a programme for monitoring, evaluating and amending the plan at regular intervals.

By-laws or local legislation, specific policies and procedures may be needed and should be properly formulated, documented and communicated to all those involved. Business and marketing plans, market research, community needs analyses and surveys of actual and potential customers should form part of the management process.

Planning for the future should advocate positive change and flexibility and aim to minimise the impact of transition on services, staff and customers. To achieve effective change, all stakeholders must be involved in the change process.

6.2.5   Green (environmentally friendly) libraries

The built environment has a vast impact on the natural environment, human health, and the economy. By adopting green building and operational strategies, public libraries can maximise both economic and environmental performance. Green construction methods can be integrated into buildings at any stage, from design and construction, to renovation and demolition. However, the most significant benefits can be obtained if the design and construction team takes an integrated approach from the earliest stages of a building project.

The World Green Building Council documents nine Green Building Rating Systems on its website <http://www.worldgbc.org/green-building-councils/green-building-rating-tools>. The countries that currently have Green Building Rating Systems are Australia, Canada, Germany, India, Japan, New Zealand, South Africa, United Kingdom, and the United States.

The Leadership in Energy and Environmental Design (LEED-INDIA) Green Building Rating System of the Indian Green Building Council promotes a whole-building approach to sustainability by recognising performance in the areas listed below. Builders choose those items that are appropriate for their project:

- Sustainable site selection and development
- Water conservation
- Energy efficiency
- Local resources, material conservation and waste reduction
- Indoor environmental quality.

Popular features incorporated into green library buildings include:

- Recycled building materials
- Low volatile organic compound (VOC) emitting paints, carpets, and adhesives
- Solar panels
- Day lighting
- Living roofs
- Rainwater harvesting.

Many libraries are incorporating green practices into their everyday operating strategies. These practices may include:

- Recycling paper and cardboard
- Composting organic materials
- Using energy efficient light bulbs
- Using nontoxic cleaning solutions.

▸ An Indiana (USA) library is built into the side of a hill and has a flat 17 250 square-foot living green roof. The soil from the hill helps the library stay cooler in the summer and warmer in the winter, and the runoff water from the roof drains into a rain garden.

▸ A library in Calgary, Alberta, Canada, incorporates natural and daylight harvesting, exterior sunshades, and on-demand water heating with low-flow plumbing fixtures to reduce the use of water and conserve energy.

▸ Energy efficiency for a USA library in Ohio will be boosted by a white roof, white concrete in the parking lot, an efficient heat-recovery system, solar shades and a lighting control system. Materials from the demolition of an existing building were recycled, including crushed concrete that went directly into the new building site.

▸ A library in Santa Monica, CA, USA, includes underground parking, solar electric panels, and a storm water management system used to irrigate the drought resistant landscape. More than 50% of the building materials contain significant recycled content. The building also uses low-flow restroom toilets and no water urinals.

6.3   Building and maintaining library networks

The library manager must ensure that networks are developed and maintained at the national, regional and local level, to ensure optimum access to ICT and cooperative services. This enables a very wide range of resources to be brought to the customer at a local level. The library manager should also develop effective working partnerships with other organisations in the community, benefiting both the library and its customers and also the partner. Examples include schools, museums and archives, other local government departments and voluntary organisations. Such partnerships confirm the public library's role at the centre of community activity. The library manager should, wherever possible, ensure that the library takes an active and positive role (such as serving as a board member) within the corporate structure of the parent organisation and within the local community.

6.4   Financial management

Financial management and financial planning are vitally important to ensure that the library operates efficiently (at optimum performance), economically (at minimum cost), and effectively (at maximum benefit). In order to achieve these aims the library manager should:

- look for ways of improving levels of funding from national, state or local government or from other sources
- prepare 3–5 year business plans based on the library's long term plans, including bids for the required funds
- allocate funds to support activities identified in the library's policy statement and based on the priorities previously determined
- establish partnerships, where appropriate, for co-operative purchasing to maximise the use of available funds
- undertake activity-based costing to determine the cost of activities and programmes and to facilitate future planning
- maintain a policy for the sustainable renewal of plants and equipment
- evaluate and implement automated techniques, wherever appropriate, to improve efficiency and effectiveness
- introduce systems that will ensure that all staff with responsibility for any part of the budget will be fully accountable for the expenditure of funds for which they are responsible
- improve staff productivity and efficiency
- develop strategies for identifying alternative sources of financial support.

6.5   Management of library resources

A major element of a library's budget is expenditure on library materials and services. The library manager should ensure that these funds are spent properly and in accordance with the agreed priorities of the library and that the materials and services are maintained and made available so that they can be of maximum benefit to the library customer.

6.6   Staff management

Library staff are a vital element of the library's resources and staff salaries are normally the largest part of the library budget. It is very important that the management of staff should be sensitive, consistent and based on sound principles if staff are to work most effectively and with high levels of motivation and job satisfaction. The following are important elements of staff management:

- An equitable procedure for staff appointments. Job and person specifications should be drawn up prior to a post being advertised. Interviews should be conducted in a way that is fair to all applicants. Appointments should be based solely on professional competence and judgment and suitability for the position and not be prejudiced by any other factors.
- Good communication between staff at all levels. Managers should review internal communication systems regularly to make sure staff are well informed about the policies and procedures of the library service.
- The opportunity for staff to participate in the development of policy and operational procedures. Initiative should be encouraged to make the best use of the skills and experience of staff. By bringing staff into the decision-making process they will feel they 'own' the policies and procedures of the service. The principles of affirmative action may also be adopted.
- Assure opportunities are available for staff training and career development.

6.7   Planning and development of library systems

To make the most effective use of resources the public library will require a variety of systems, for example circulation control, financial management, internal communications and online access to the Internet. The library manager should ensure that appropriate systems are introduced, making use of specialist staff for their development where necessary. Staff must be given adequate training in the use of such systems, the effectiveness of which must be reviewed regularly.

6.8   The management of change

In common with many other organisations public libraries are going through a period of unprecedented and ongoing change as a result of the rapid development of information technology and social and demographic change. This presents tremendous opportunities for the public library, as information provision is one of its primary roles. It also presents challenges to managers and staff to ensure that change can be introduced with the maximum effectiveness and the least stress on staff and the organisation. Library managers must be aware of the issues arising from continuous and fundamental change and establish methods of dealing with them.

6.8.1   Planning for the future

Library managers should be aware of developments both within and outside librarianship that are likely to have an impact on service development. They should make time to read and study so that they can anticipate the effect of changes, particularly technological, on the future shape of the service. They should also ensure that policy-makers and other staff are kept informed of future developments.

6.9   Delegation

The library manager in charge of the public library service has ultimate responsibility for the service, in conjunction with the governing body. However, all library staff with responsibility for any resources of the library, whether materials, staff or library premises, have a managerial role, and this should be recognised by the library manager and the member of staff concerned. They should be given appropriate managerial training and participate in the policy development of the library whenever possible. Managerial responsibility should be delegated to staff at an appropriate lower level. It should be made clear what responsibilities are being delegated and the reporting mechanism to senior managers. Staff must be given training to enable them to carry out the delegated responsibilities effectively. A planned system of delegation makes best use of the skills and experience of a wide range of staff and provides opportunities for professional development. It also increases the number of people fully involved in the development and operation of the library service, improves job satisfaction and prepares staff for promotion when opportunities arise.

6.10   Management tools

A wide range of management tools can be used in a public library. Their relevance will depend on a number of factors, for example, the cultural context, the size and character of the service, the management style of other departments in the same organisation and available experience and funding. The following are however important tools for public libraries in almost any situation:
– environmental scanning
– community needs analysis
– monitoring and evaluation
– performance measurement.

> ▶ The Public Reading Map of Catalonia, Spain is a planning tool for the public library system, identifying requirements for library facilities and subsequent types of services most desirable based upon the population and core demographics.
> <http://cultura.gencat.cat/biblio/mapa/>

6.10.1 Environmental scanning

Marketers often define the internal environment as the "microenvironment." This internal environment must work in partnership with the external environment. The more cognisant the organisation is of this relationship the more proactively it can respond to change. The environment that the library resides within and the materials and services that the library offers, ultimately affect the end users who are the library's customers. The larger environment which is built upon those forces outside the library's control is called the external or "macro environment." These external forces can originate from local, regional, national or international levels. These forces include the state of the economy; the geographical characteristics and infrastructure; competition; legal and political restrictions and issues; technological developments; the media; natural resources; and the ever changing social and cultural conditions.

The process of gathering information from these categories aforementioned is in fact the process of "environmental scanning." During this activity, management is constantly identifying strengths and weaknesses in the internal organisation, as well as opportunities and threats from the external environment. Collectively, this is often called the SWOT list: assessing the strengths, weaknesses, opportunities, and threats of an organisation and its environment. This scanning, gathering of critical and relevant data, and the SWOT review, results in the best opportunity to understand what factors facilitate offering optimal products and services that meet the specified needs and desires of the library's customers.

6.10.2 Community needs analysis

In order to provide services that meet the needs of the whole community, the public library has to establish the extent of those needs. As needs and expectations will change, this process will need to be repeated at regular intervals, perhaps every five years. A community needs assessment is a process in which the library collects detailed information about the local community and its library and information needs. Planning and policy development are based on the results of this assessment and in this way a match between services and needs can be achieved. In some countries the preparation of a community needs assessment is a legislative requirement of the local authority. The information to be collected will include:

- socio-demographic information about the local community e.g., the age and gender profile, ethnic diversity, educational level
- data about organisations in the community, e.g., educational institutions, health centres, hospitals, penal establishments, voluntary organisations
- information about business and commerce in the locality
- the catchment area of the library, i.e. where library users live in relation to the library
- transport patterns in the community
- information services provided by other agencies in the community.

This is not an exhaustive list and further research would be required to establish what information is needed to form a community needs assessment in each situation. However, the principle of preparing a community profile, which will enable the librarian and the governing body to plan service development and promotion on the needs of the community, is an important one whatever the local context. The assessment should be complemented by regular customer surveys to establish what library and information services the public wants, at what level, and how they judge the services they receive. Survey work is a specialist skill and, where resources are available, a more objective result will be gained if the survey is carried out by an external organisation.

6.10.3 Monitoring and evaluation

As the library service moves towards its goals, management must be accountable in terms of financial control and the monitoring and evaluation of library activities. Management must continually monitor the performance of the library service to ensure that strategies and operational results are achieving the set objectives. Statistics should be collected over time to allow trends to be identified. Community needs and satisfaction surveys, and performance indicators are valuable tools in monitoring the achievements of the library. Techniques should be developed to measure the quality of the services provided and their impact on the community. All programmes and services should be evaluated on a regular basis to ascertain whether they are:

- achieving the objectives and declared goals of the library
- actually and regularly provided
- meeting the needs of the community
- able to meet changing needs
- in need of improvement, new direction or redefinition
- adequately resourced
- cost effective.

Procedures and processes operating within the library also require constant evaluation and revision to increase efficiency and effectiveness. An outside evaluation and audit is also valuable to assure accountability to the commmunity served and funders.

6.10.4 Performance indicators

The availability of reliable performance information is a necessary tool for evaluation and the improvement of efficiency, effectiveness and quality of service (performance measurement). The collection of statistics related to resources, staff, services, circulation, activities etc. will provide data for planning, show accountability and assist informed management decision-making. The indicators should be kept up to date.

The following key performance indicators may be used to evaluate and monitor the achievement of the library's objectives.

Usage indicators

- loans per capita
- total library visits per capita
- membership as a percentage of the population
- loans per item, i.e. turnover resources
- reference and electronic reference enquiries per capita
- loans per opening hour
- number of accesses to electronic services and other non-print materials
- website visits
- comparative data for example, of print and non-print materials
- dowloaded materials, e.g. podcasts
- booking meeting spaces
- registrants vs. active registrants
- number of items placed on hold and percentage of these requests filled from the collection.

Resource indicators

- total stock per capita
- provision of online public access computers (OPACs) per capita.

Human resource indicators

- ratio of full time equivalent (FTE) staff to population
- ratio of professional staff to population
- ratio of full time equivalent (FTE) staff to any library usage indicator.

Qualitative indicators

- customer satisfaction surveys
- enquiries satisfied.

Cost indicators

- unit costs for functions, services and activities
- staff costs per functions, e.g., books processed, programmes
- total costs per capita, per member, per visitor, per service point etc.

Comparative indicators

- bench-mark statistical data against other relevant and comparable library services, internationally, nationally and locally.

In addition to the collection and analysis of input and output service statistics, the unstated needs of potential customers should be established by carrying out market research including the use of focus groups and community surveys.

Where reliable population statistics are not available it becomes more difficult to develop reliable performance indicators. Use can be made of estimated population totals, the comparison of costs with customer and visitor statistics and bench-marking with other libraries with similar characteristics.

6.10.5 Performance measurement

Performance measurement has been used in public libraries for some years. Measurements or performance indicators are established to measure the input to libraries, that is the resources devoted to the whole or particular services, and the output: what is achieved as a result of the activity being carried out. For example, the establishment of an enquiry service for customers requires the input of staff, materials, equipment and floor space. The output is the number of enquiries received, the number satisfied, the level of use made of the resources and the use of other services, for example, the reservation service, arising from the original activity. These measures can then be compared each year to see if the effectiveness of the library service is improving.

In the past few years an additional measure has become standard for many libraries, the outcome measure. An outcome measure is a measure of change (or lack of change) in the well-being of a defined customer population. For example, a library may provide homework assistance and tutoring services to school students. The input measure would include the number of books or tutors available, the output would be the hours of tutoring or books circulated and the outcome measure would be the level of improvement of the student's school grades or the student's perception of their increased knowledge.

Computer technology makes performance measurement a simpler task and enables sophisticated models of library use to be established and used in service development. Performance measurement should be a planned process carried out with consistency over a period of time. Further information about library performance indicators can be found in ISO 11620:2008 *Information and documentation. Library performance indicators.*

Another way of gaining a useful indication of the success of a library service is to compare key input and output measurements with other public libraries of similar size and characteristics. This is usually known as bench-marking and is a useful adjunct to performance measurements carried out internally.

Resources

Brophy, P. (2006). *Measuring library performance: principles and techniques*. London: Facet.

Bryan, C. (2007). *Managing facilities for results: Optimizing space for services*. Chicago: American Library Association.

Chicago Public Library, Chicago Public Library Foundation, Board Steering Committee, and Boston Consulting Group. (n.d.). *Chicago Public Library 2010: A vision for our future*. (http://www.chipublib.org/dir_documents/cpl2010.pdf accessed 1/01/2010).

Dowlin, K. (2009). *Getting the money: How to succeed in fundraising for public and nonprofit libraries*. Westport, CT: Libraries Unlimited.

Elliott, D. S., Holt, G.E., Hayden, S.W., and Holt, L.E. (2007). *Measuring your library's value: How to do a cost-benefit analysis for your public library*. Chicago: American Library Association.

Herring, M. (2004). *Raising funds with friends groups*. New York: Neal Schuman.

Hughes, K. M. (2009). *The PLA Reader for public library directors and managers*. New York: Neal-Schuman.

IFLA. (n.d.) *Professional codes of ethics for librarians*. (http://www.ifla.org/en/faife/professional-codes-of-ethics-for-librarians accessed 1/01/2010).

Institute of Museum and Library Services (n.d.) Public library data files. (http://harvester.census.gov/imls/data/pls/index.asp accessed 3/15/2010.)

Landau, H. B. (2008). *The small public library survival guide*. Chicago: American Library Association.

Matthews, J. R. (2008). *Scorecard for results: A guide for developing a library balanced scorecard*. Westport, CT: Libraries Unlimited.

Nelson, S. S. (2009). *Implementing for results: Your strategic plan in action*. Chicago: American Library Association.

Rubin, R. J. (2006). *Demonstrating for results: Using outcome measurement in your library*. Chicago: American Library Association.

United States Environmental Protection Agency. (n.d.). *Why build green?* (http://www.epa.gov/greenbuilding/pubs/whybuild.htm accessed 1/01/2010).

7

The marketing of public libraries

7.1   Introduction

Marketing is much more than advertising, selling, persuasion or promotion. Marketing is a tried and true systematic approach that relies on designing the service or product in terms of the customers' needs and desires, with satisfaction as its goal.

7.2   Marketing tools

The marketing function is the driving force of any successful business or library and is comprised of four major tools. These include: 1) marketing research; 2) marketing segmentation; 3) the marketing mix strategy (the 4 P's – product, price, place and promotion); and 4) marketing evaluation. Library managers can use these marketing tools to identify and understand the needs of their customers and plan to effectively meet their needs.

7.2.1   Marketing research

Marketing research is a planning process of finding out all about the library's markets. A market or the ideal potential market is all the people who have some stated interest in a particular product or service or could be expected to do so. The internal records of the library contain valuable market information about actual customers including: circulation data which might provide the geographic residence of customers as well as age, sex and type of reading material checked out. Other use data may include number and type of reference questions, and online searches performed and the subjects of the searches.

Market research of society as a whole, regarding potential customer demographics, trends in health, sexual mores, entertainment and sports, are all important in assessing the information, education and entertainment needs of the library's population. This information is useful if not essential for developing the library's collection of services and materials and programmes. Library managers must be cognisant of legal aspects of customer data.

▸ Ohio Library Council
<http://www.olc.org/marketing/index.html> offers six different modules that are entitled overview, planning, product, promotion, Internet, and Ohio.
▸ Webjunction <http://www.webjunction.org/marketing> is an online resource offering expertise on marketing related topics for library and information professionals.
▸ North Suburban Library, USA website
<http://www.nsls.info/resources/marketing/> includes articles on marketing generalizable to any library. There are podcasts, sample marketing plans, and a toolkit.
▸ The US Public Library Geographic Database is a free Internet-based map of US public library locations and customer data.
<http://geolib.org/PLGDB.cfm>

7.2.2 Marketing segmentation

The second step marketing tool which is necessarily based upon marketing research is segmentation. A market segment is a group of potential customers who share similar wants and needs. Market segmentation is based on the fact that markets are heterogeneous. It is imperative for library managers to define and understand various markets in order to allocate resources efficiently and to provide services effectively.

Libraries segment customer markets in a variety of ways. By materials and services, for example fiction readers, storyhour attendees, genealogy enthusiasts, online customers. Or perhaps by age groups, such as young adults, juveniles, adults, the elderly. By contrast a university typically segments by field of study, or class level – freshmen, sophomore, junior, senior, graduate student – or by faculty, staff or community member.

The private sector learned long ago that treating all customers the same may achieve profit on some levels. But they also learned when the differences of customers within the market are ignored, the result may be that no one is really getting what they want and need from a product or service designed for a mass market.

7.2.3   Marketing mix strategy

Most organisations (libraries included) offer limited resources and therefore must allocate these resources accordingly. For example, the reference service must support the goals and objectives of the library. But it must also meet (or attempt to meet) the needs of every individual that accesses the website, calls in or walks in. Therefore, this third step of the marketing model which develops product, price, place and promotion [4 Ps] of materials and services and programmes based upon market research to various market segments assists the libraries in utilising these limited funds in an efficient and effective manner. While the mix is the most visible part of the marketing model, it is not exclusively the most important.

Librarians historically participate heavily in the promotion arm of the mix. Promotion is sometimes confused with public relations which is a two-way communication that depends on feedback. Promotion simply articulates what the library is doing and what it is. Little explicit regard is typically given to the rest of the mix strategy including aspects of price (sum of cost to customers); place (of delivery i.e., branches, website); and products (books, computer access, librarian assistance and other services) when considering which segments to prioritise service to.

▸ LibraryJournal.com contains the Bubble Room <http://www.libraryjournal.com/blog/820000682.html> providing many links to various timely marketing articles that focus on library marketing.
▸ KnowThis.com's free *Principles of Marketing* tutorial series focuses on the key concepts and functions that are common to most marketing situations no matter what an organisation's size, industry, geographic location. <http://www.knowthis.com/principles-of-marketing-tutorials/>
▸ American Marketing Association (AMA) <http://www.marketingpower.com> includes AMA Publications,

articles, webcasts, podcasts, directories, and journals. It is searchable by topic, phrase, date, author, or content source. Because one of the primary goals of the AMA is to educate and train future marketers, much of this information is available for free online.

▸ The "M" Word – Marketing Libraries is authored by Nancy Dowd and Kathy Dempsey. <http://themwordblog.blogspot.com/index.html.> This blog helps librarians understand how to optimally market their library, and is regularly updated with stories and information focusing on tips and tricks for marketing the unique aspects of libraries.

▸ "Marketing-mantra-for-librarians" is a blog authored by Dinesh Gupta, India, offering advice and tips on library marketing and user-focused services. <http://marketing-mantra-for-librarians.blogspot.com/>

7.2.4   Promotion plan

To enable the library to achieve its marketing strategy, a coherent promotional plan should be developed. It could include the following elements:

- making positive use of print, electronic and communications media
- links to and from related websites and portals
- library websites, podcasts and RSS feeds
- social media such as Facebook, Twitter and YouTube
- regular publications and the preparation of resource lists and pamphlets
- displays and exhibits
- effective interior and exterior sign-posting
- book fairs
- friends of the library groups
- annual library week celebrations and other collective promotional activities
- special years of celebration and anniversaries
- fund-raising activities and campaigns
- public-speaking activities and liaison with community groups
- reading and literacy campaigns
- designing campaigns to meet the needs of people with physical and sensory disabilities
- library listings in the telephone book and other community directories
- web links to other community agencies/directories

- special library publications, e.g., history of the library, or community
- special reports designed for the public and local government

This list is not exhaustive and other elements can be added depending on local circumstances and customer segment use of specific media.

7.2.5   Marketing evaluation

Marketing evaluation includes two major methods. One is assessing customer behaviour (i.e. how many signed up for virtual reference, what time of day are questions most often asked, which subject areas are most popular?) The other attempts to measure customer satisfaction (i.e. how well does the service meet customer needs, what benefits are received, and how likely are they to use the service again?) The first process also requires gathering internal customer data, while the latter activity, that of measuring customer satisfaction, can only come from data gathered by asking customers questions through personal interview, online or print survey, focus groups, and other methodologies.

> ▶ Sponsored by the Graduate School of Library and Information Science, University of Illinois at Urbana-Champaign, USA, this site offers citations to articles, books, marketing strategies, and examples of how to best communicate with diverse populations. Web resources are available directing the reader to best marketing practices of libraries.
> <http://clips.lis.uiuc.edu/2003_09.html>

7.3   Marketing and communications policy

The library should have a written communications, marketing and promotions policy to enable it to undertake planned programmes of same to the public. The policy should include considerations of any legal factors; stated responsibilities for media interaction; technology barriers or opportunities; appropriate written and oral communication methods; and overall marketing and communication strategies of the organisation which facilitate the mission.

> ▶ Libraries are accessing social media to engage customers, and necessarily developing specialized policies and procedures. Examples of these policies are cited.
> <http://www.schoollibraryjournal.com/article/CA6699104.html>

7.4   Public relations

Public relations (PR) is the practice of managing the flow of information between a library and its community. Public relations gains the library exposure to their community and customer markets using topics of interest and news items that do not require direct payment. Effective PR includes successful relationshps with media personnel and community groups and leaders.

▸ CanalBib, is a Youtube selection, offering videos related to library PR and library customers.
<http://www.youtube.com/user/canalbib>
▸ In Spain the initiative 'Nascuts per llegir' (Born to read) introduces library services to children ages 0 to 3 years by strengthening parent-child love of books and libraries. The initiative was developed by the Professional Catalan Association to promote reading amongst families.
<http://nascutsperllegir.org>

7.4.1   Working with the media

Library staff should be trained to use communication media to promote the library service and respond to media enquiries. They should be able to write articles for local newspapers and prepare press releases. They should be familiar with the techniques of speaking and being interviewed on radio and television. They should also be able to promote the library and its services via computer and telecommunication networks including the creation of library websites and the development of library blogs, podcasts, RSS feeds and use of social media.

7.4.2   Community support

The library managers must ensure that the community is aware of the importance of the library service. Municipal, regional and national funding bodies should be made fully aware of the important place that the library occupies in the community, and support its development.

7.4.3   Gaining community support

The library should have an agreed policy and a sustained programme for developing community support. This can include:

- maintaining a 'friends of the library' organisation for fund-raising and general support
- working with community advocates in support of major initiatives such as new buildings and services
- forming liaisons with community groups to enhance parts of the collection or strengthen specific services
- working with groups that wish to speak out on behalf of the library service and its development
- participation by library staff in activities aimed at increasing awareness of the variety and value of the library service.

The support of the community also depends on the library delivering the services it has promised to deliver.

7.4.4 Advocacy

The library should have established and adopted written policies that define its role in generating public support for the library service.

A well informed public can provide valuable support for the public library service and actively promote it within the community. Getting people to talk positively about the library and its services is one of the most effective marketing tools. Lobbying involves interaction with decision-makers to secure specific objectives at an appropriate point in the legislative, policy-making or budget process.

7.4.5 Working with governing bodies

Library managers should meet at least annually with the library's principal governing and funding body to review the library's services, development plans, achievements and obstacles. Librarians should look for as many opportunities as possible to involve its governing body in its major activities. Events such as the opening of a new library, the launching of a service, the installation of public Internet access, the opening of a new collection and the inauguration of a fund-raising drive can be used for this purpose.

7.4.6 Participation in community life

One of the most effective promotional strategies is the participation of well-informed library staff and committee or board members in community activities. Examples include:

- presenting book and activity reviews on radio and television
- working with adult and children's literature and cultural groups
- writing a newspaper column
- supporting literacy organisations and campaigns
- participating in the activities of local organisations
- assisting with school-based initiatives
- participating in local history and genealogy societies
- being a member of a service organisation, e.g., Rotary International
- visiting local organisations to promote the library service.

Resources

12manage. (n.d.) *12manage: The executive fast track.*
(http://www.12manage.com/management_views.asp
accessed 1/01/2010).

Dempsey, K. (2009). *The accidental library marketer.* Medford, NJ: Information Today.

Dowd, N; Evangeliste, M; and Silberman, J. (2009). *Bite-sized marketing: realistic solutions for the overworked librarian.* Chicago: ALA Editions.

Fisher, P. H., Pride, M. M., and Miller, E.G. (2006). *Blueprint for your library marketing plan: A guide to help you survive and thrive.* Chicago: American Library Association.

Flaten, T. (2006). *Management, marketing and promotion of library services based on statistics, analyses and evaluation.* Munich: K.G. Saur.

Gupta, D. (2006). *Marketing library and information services: International perspectives.* Munich: K.G. Suar.

Gupta, D. (n.d.). *Marketing-mantra-for-librarians: Library marketing: Imperative to user-focused services in your library.*
(http://marketing-mantra-for-librarians.blogspot.com/
accessed 1/01/2010).

Kendrick, T. (2006). *Developing strategic marketing plans that really work: A toolkit for public libraries.* London: Facet.

Koontz, C.M. (2002-2009). *Customer-based marketing columns.* Medford, NJ: Information Today. Some issues are online
(http://www.infotoday.com/MLS/default.shtml
accessed 3/27/2010).

Koontz, C.M. (2001). *Glossary of marketing definitions: IFLA Section on Management and Marketing.* (http://archive.ifla.org/VII/s34/pubs/glossary.htm> accessed 3/9/2010.)

Kujawski, M. (2008). *What would happen if the STOP sign was invented in 2008? Public Sector Marketing 2.0.* (http://www.mikekujawski.ca/2008/12/17/what-would-happen-if-the-stop-sign-was-invented-in-2008/ accessed 1/01/2010).

Lake, Laura. (2009). *Understanding the Role of Social Media in Marketing.* (http://marketing.about.com/od/strategytutorials/a/socialmediamktg.htm accessed 3/15/2009).

Online Computer Library Center, Inc. (OCLC). (2005). *Perceptions of Libraries and Information Resources.* (http://www.oclc.org/reports/2005perceptions.htm accessed 1/01/2010).

Savard, R. (2000). *Adapting marketing to libraries in a changing and world-wide environment.* Munich: K.G. Saur.

Wolfe, L. A. (2005). *Library public relations, promotions, communications: A how to do it manual.* New York: Neal Schuman Publishers.

Woodward, J. (2005). *Creating the customer-driven library: Building on the bookstore model.* Chicago: American Library Association.

Wymer. W. (2006). *Nonprofit marketing: Marketing management for charitable and non-governmental organizations.* Thousand Oaks, CA.: Sage Publications, Inc.

Appendix 1

The IFLA/UNESCO Public Library Manifesto

A Gateway to Knowledge

Freedom, prosperity and the development of society and of individuals are fundamental human values. They will only be attained through the ability of well-informed citizens to exercise their democratic rights and to play an active role in society. Constructive participation and the development of democracy depend on satisfactory education as well as on free and unlimited access to knowledge, thought, culture and information.

The public library, the local gateway to knowledge, provides a basic condition for lifelong learning, independent decision-making and cultural development of the individual and social groups.

This Manifesto proclaims UNESCO's belief in the public library as a living force for education, culture and information, and as an essential agent for the fostering of peace and spiritual welfare through the minds of men and women.

UNESCO therefore encourages national and local governments to support and actively engage in the development of public libraries.

The Public Library

The public library is the local centre of information, making all kinds of knowledge and information readily available to its users.

The services of the public library are provided on the basis of equality of access for all, regardless of age, race, sex, religion, nationality, language or social status. Specific services and materials must be provided for those users who cannot, for whatever reason, use the regular services and materials, for example linguistic minorities, people with disabilities or people in hospital or prison.

All age groups must find material relevant to their needs. Collections and services have to include all types of appropriate media and modern technologies as well as traditional materials. High quality and relevance to local needs and conditions are fundamental. Material must reflect current trends and the evolution of society, as well as the memory of human endeavour and imagination.

Collections and services should not be subject to any form of ideological, political or religious censorship, nor commercial pressures.

Missions of the Public Library

Missions of the public library. The following key missions which relate to information, literacy, education and culture should be at the core of public library services:

1 creating and strengthening reading habits in children from an early age;
2 supporting both individual and self conducted education as well as formal education at all levels;
3 providing opportunities for personal creative development;
4 stimulating the imagination and creativity of children and young people;
5 promoting awareness of cultural heritage, appreciation of the arts, scientific achievements and innovations;
6 providing access to cultural expressions of all performing arts;
7 fostering inter-cultural dialogue and favouring cultural diversity;
8 supporting the oral tradition;
9 ensuring access for citizens to all sorts of community information;
10 providing adequate information services to local enterprises, associations and interest groups;
11 facilitating the development of information and computer literacy skills;
12 supporting and participating in literary activities and programmes for all age groups, and initiating such activities if necessary.

Funding, legislation and networks

The public library shall in principle be free of charge. The public library is the responsibility of local and national authorities. It must be supported by specific legislation and financed by national and local government. It has to be an essential component of any long-term strategy for culture, information provision, literacy and education.

To ensure nationwide library coordination and cooperation, legislation and strategic plans must also define and promote a national library network based on agreed standards of service

The public library network must be designed in relation to national, regional, research and special libraries as well as libraries in schools, colleges and universities.

Operation and management

A clear policy must be formulated, defining objectives, priorities and services in relation to the local community needs. The public library has to be organized effectively and professional standards of operation must be maintained.

Cooperation with relevant partners-for example, user groups and other professionals at local, regional, national as well as international levels has to be ensured.

Services have to be physically accessible to all members of the community. This requires well situated library buildings, good reading and study facilities, as well as relevant technologies and sufficient opening hours convenient to the users. It equally implies outreach services for those unable to visit the library.

The library services must be adapted to the different needs of communities in rural and urban areas.

The librarian is an active intermediary between users and resources. Professional and continuing education of the librarian is indispensable to ensure adequate services.

Outreach and user education programmes have to be provided to help users benefit from all the resources.

Implementing the Manifesto

Decision makers at national and local levels and the library community at large, around the world, are hereby urged to implement the principles expressed in this Manifesto.

This Manifesto is prepared in cooperation with the International Federation of Library Associations and Institutions (IFLA).

The Manifesto can be seen in over twenty languages on the IFLA web-site: http://www.ifla.org/VII/s8/unesco/manif.htm

Appendix 2

The Finnish Library Act (904/1998)

Issued in Helsinki on the 4th of December 1998
In accordance with a decision of Parliament the following is enacted

Chapter 1   Objectives

1. This act prescribes the library and information services to be provided by municipal public libraries, and the promotion of these services both nationally and regionally.

2. The objective of the library and information services provided by public libraries is to promote equal opportunities among citizens for personal cultivation, for literary and cultural pursuits, for continuous development of knowledge, personal skills and civic skills, for internationalisation, and for lifelong learning.

Library activities also aim at promoting the development of virtual and interactive network services and their educational and cultural contents.

Chapter 2   Arranging library and information services

3. The municipality shall be responsible for arranging the library and information services referred to in this act.

The municipality may provide the library and information services independently, or partly or totally in co-operation with other municipalities, or in any other way. The municipality is responsible for the services being in accordance with this act.

Library users shall have access to library and information professionals, and to continually renewing library material and equipment.

In a bilingual municipality, the needs of both language groups shall be taken into consideration on equal grounds

In the municipalities of the Saami home area, the needs of both the Saami and the Finnish language groups shall be taken into consideration on equal grounds.

Chapter 3   The library and information service network

4. A public library shall operate in co-operation with other public libraries, with research libraries and with libraries in educational establishments, as part of the national and international networks of library and information services.

The libraries acting as the central library for public libraries and as provincial libraries supplement the services of public libraries.

The central library for public libraries is a public library in a municipality appointed by the relevant ministry, with the consent of the municipality. Its sphere of operations shall be the whole country.

A provincial library is a public library in a municipality appointed by the relevant ministry, with the consent of the municipality. The sphere of operations shall be laid down by the relevant ministry.

The tasks of the central library and the provincial library shall be enacted in a decree. The relevant ministry can, after consulting the municipality, cancel the designation as central or a provincial library.

Chapter 4   Library services free of charge

5. The use of the library's own collections within the library and borrowing from them shall be free of charge.

Inter-library loans issued by the central library and by the provincial libraries to public libraries shall be free of charge.

For other library transactions, the municipality may charge a fee amounting to the prime cost of the transaction at most.

For a specific reason, the fee which would otherwise be fixed to amount to the prime cost may exceed this.

Chapter 5 Evaluation

6. The municipality shall evaluate the library and information service it provides.

The purpose of the evaluation is to improve access to library and information services and to promote their development. The evaluation shall monitor the implementation of the library and information services and the quality and cost-effectiveness of the services.

Each municipality is obliged to take part in evaluation referred to by this clause.

Decisions about national evaluation and about national participation in international evaluations shall be made by the relevant ministry, which shall carry out the evaluation together with the Provincial State Offices.

The municipality shall contribute to the evaluation referred to in this subsection.

Salient findings of the evaluation shall be made public.

Chapter 6 State administration of library and information services

7. The relevant ministry shall be the national administrator for library and information services. The provincial state office shall be the regional administrative authority. The tasks of the provincial state office shall be enacted in a decree.

Chapter 7 Miscellaneous regulations

8. The library system shall have a sufficient number of staff qualified for library and information service and other personnel.
The qualification requirements for library staff shall be enacted in a decree.
For a specific reason, the relevant ministry may grant exception from the formal qualification requirements.

9. The municipality shall receive statutory state aid towards the cost of operating the library under the Act on the Financing of Educational and Cultural Provision (635/1998).

The municipality shall receive a government grant towards the costs of constructing and renovating a library under the Act on the Financing of Educational and Cultural Provision. The purchase of a mobile library bus or boat shall also be regarded as construction.

10. The library may issue library rules which contain provisions concerning the use of the library and the rights and duties of the library user.

Infringement of the library rules shall be chargeable with fines commensurate with the infringement.

11. More detailed provisions on the application of this act shall be issued by statute.

THE FINNISH LIBRARY DECREE (1078/998)

Issued at Helsinki on 18th December 1998

Section 1 Functions of the Central Library of Public Libraries

The central library of public libraries shall

1. act as the national interlibrary lending centre
2. promote co-operation of public libraries and between public and scientific libraries
3. develop common methods and instruments necessary for organising library and information services
4. perform other duties assigned by the competent Ministry.

Section 2 Functions of a Provincial Library

A Provincial Library shall

1. support the information and interlibrary lending services of the public libraries within its region
2. develop information services relating to its own sphere of operation
3. provide the personnel of the sphere of operation with training in new forms and development projects of library work
4. perform other duties assigned by the competent Ministry.

Section 3   Functions of the State Provincial Office

The State Provincial Office shall

1. in co-operation with the competent Ministry, monitor and promote library and information services needed by the population, and evaluate the accessibility and quality of the services
2. promote regional, national and international development projects in the field of library and information service
3. perform other duties assigned by the competent Ministry.

Section 4   Qualification Requirements

A minimum of two thirds of the personnel referred to in Section 8, Subsection 1 of the Library Act (904/1998), must have a university degree, or college diploma, or a vocational qualification which includes, or has been supplemented with, a minimum of 20 credits of library and information studies at a university or a vocational institution.

The qualification required from the person responsible for the library and information services in a municipality shall be a higher university degree which includes, or has been supplemented with, a minimum of 35 credits of library and information studies.

Section 5   Entry into Force

The Decree shall come into force on the first day of January 1999.

The provisions of Section 4, Subsection 1 shall not apply to the personnel employed by a library at the time when this Decree comes into force.

Any process of filling a vacant post or position pending at the time when this Decree comes into force shall be subject to / comply with the qualification requirements valid prior to the entry into force of this Decree.

Before the entry into force of this Decree, necessary measures may be taken to implement it.

Section 6 Transitional Provisions concerning Personnel

Not detailed here

Section 7 Transitional Provisions concerning the Completion of Studies

Not detailed here

Appendix 3

Customer charter

A number of public library services have prepared customer/user charters. The following example is from Buckinghamshire County Library, England.
http://www.buckscc.gov.uk/bcc/libraries/customer_charter.page

Buckinghamshire County Library
Library Service Customer Charter

We want everyone in Buckinghamshire to receive a high quality service. Our charter sets out the standards we aim to achieve. It also tells you what to do if you want our service to change or improve.

Accessible and welcoming

- Library access and membership is free to all.
- The Centre for Buckinghamshire Studies and the Buckinghamshire County Museum are both free to visit.
- Our network of 27 libraries and six mobile libraries means that 99% of households are within one mile of a library service. Items can be borrowed, returned or renewed at any library.
- Opening times are planned to meet the needs of local communities. We will consult local people before making any changes.
- Our services will reflect the cultural and linguistic diversity of local communities.
- All our premises have ramped or level access, and are equipped with a hearing loop. We are committed to making our services fully accessible to people with disabilities. Our staff have received Disability Awareness Training and are always pleased to provide assistance.
- We will provide a delivered Home Library Service for anyone who is unable to visit a library in person, owing to age, illness or disability.

A quality service

- You will be served by helpful and courteous staff wearing identity badges, who have received training in customer care.
- 98% of our customers will be served within 3 minutes of beginning to wait.
- Our libraries will supply 50% of requested books and other items within 7 days, 72% within 15 days, and 85% within 30 days.

Consultation and feedback

- Your ideas and opinions will help us improve our services. You can speak to a manager, fill in a Customer Comment Form, or contact us by letter (Head of Service, Culture and Learning, Buckingham-shire County Council., County Hall, Aylesbury, Bucks HP20 1UU) or email on library@buckscc.gov.uk;museum@buckscc.gov.uk; archives@buckscc.gov.uk.
- We will acknowledge or reply to formal complaints within 3 work-ing days. You will receive a full reply within 10 working days, but if further investigation is required, you will be informed how long this will take.
- Our Complaints Procedure is displayed in every library, the County Museum and the Centre for Buckinghamshire Studies.
- We will survey the satisfaction levels of adults and children using all our services at least every 2 years, and publish the results.

Our performance will be checked against the standards in this charter, and the results published.

For more information call 0845 2303232 or email library@buckscc.gov.uk

Appendix 4

Library Building Standards – Ontario, Canada and Barcelona, Spain

There is no universal standard of measurement for public library buildings. However standards have been developed in some countries or regions. As examples, which may be useful when planning a library building, standards used by Ontario, Canada and Barcelona, Spain are included in this appendix. It is important that the unique needs of any community must be a primary factor in determining the final space allocated for the library. The examples in this appendix should be used in conjunction with all the sections of Paragraph 3.10 Library Buildings.

Library planners should keep in mind that automation has changed library services patterns and the design and size of the library must take current and future technology into account.

Ontario Public Library Guidelines 1997

The following methods are used by Ontario Public Libraries to determine floor-space requirements.

1. **Average square feet per capita.** For a community under 100 000 population the appropriate standard is 56 sq. m. (600 sq. ft.) per 1000 capita

2. **Building size determined by major components.**
(1) Collection space: Collection space can be determined by using the average standard of 110 volumes per sq. m. (10.8 sq. ft.) This allows for low shelving and wider aisles in specialized areas such as children's and reference collections, with regular shelving and aisle allocations in the larger non-fiction area.

Space required = 1 sq. m. (10.8 sq. ft.) for every 110 volumes.

(2) User space: An acceptable standard for user space in a library is 5 user spaces per 1000 capita. This allows for individual study stations in adult and children's areas, as well as informal seating, reference tables, A/V stations, public Internet stations.

A space of 2.8 sq. m. (30 sq. ft.) for each reader station is an acceptable standard.

(3) Staff space: A recommended library standard used to determine the number of staff is 1 staff member per 2000 population (See also Paragraph 5.6). Staff space can be determined by using a total space per staff member of 16.3 sq. m. (175 sq. ft.) This figure includes work-stations, reader services desks, circulation areas, lounge, locker facilities, etc.

Space required: 16.3 sq. m. (175 sq. ft.) per staff member @ 1 staff member per 2000 population.

(4) Multi-purpose rooms: Each library should assign space for these rooms based on community service and programme objectives.

(5) Non-assignable space: Non-assignable space includes washrooms, janitorial space, mechanical, elevators, staircases, etc. The need for non-assignable space is reduced where the library shares washrooms, mechanical areas etc. with another tenant in one building.

Space required = 20% of net space (i.e. 20% of the total of items (1) to (4)).

(6) Minimum overall size
The minimum size for an independent library should not be less than 370 sq. m. (4000 sq. ft.).

In a multi-branch system, the branch should have not less than 230 sq. m. (2500 sq. ft.) of floor space plus 14 sq. m. (150 sq. ft.) for each additional 1000 volumes over 3000 volumes in its collection.

Ontario Public Library Guidelines: a development tool for small, medium and country libraries, Sudbury, Ontario, Ontario Library Service North, 1997.

Diputació de Barcelona Library Service: Basic Public Library Standards Revised March 1999

Pop.	Branch Library — Towns 3000–5000	Public Library — Towns 5000–10 000	Towns 10–20 000	Towns 20–30 000	Central Library — Towns 30–50 000	Towns over 50 000	County Library — Towns up to 50 000	Towns over 50 000
PREMISES, m²								
Public Areas								
Lobby	15–15	15–30	30–40	40–60	60–110	110–150	60–110	110–150
Multi-purpose Hall	–50	50–60	60–80	80–100	100–150	150–200	100–150	150–200
General Area: Lending	130–200	200–270	270–410	410–645	645–930	930–1450	580–930	930–1450
Reference								
Magazines/Audiovisuals	60–90	90–100	100–115	115–140	140–250	250–400	110–250	250–400
Children's Area	60–90	90–120	120–160	160–225	225–300	300–360	180–300	300–360
Areas Reserved for Staff								
Office	15–15	15–20	20–20	20–30	30–40	40–100	50–65	65–180
Storeroom	20–30	30–40	40–60	60–80	80–150	150–230	115–210	210–350
Rest Area	–10	10–10	10–15	15–20	20–30	30–35	20–35	35–40
Car Park					–40	40–75	75–150	150–170
Programme Area	300–500	500–650	650–900	900–1300	1300–2000	2000–3000	1300–2200	2200–3300
Service Areas								
Cleaning Facilities								
Corridors, etc.	The total built area is the programme area plus 30%							
Toilet Facilities								
Total Built Area	390–650	650–845	845–1170	1170–1690	1690–2600	2600–3900	1690–2860	2860–4290
FACILITIES								
Places for Reading, Audiovisuals and Computer Work (number of places)								
General Area	20–30	30–40	40–60	60–85	85–115	115–145	50–115	115–145
Children's Area	15–20	20–25	25–35	35–50	50–65	65–75	40–65	65–75
Magazines: Table	2–4	4–4	4–6	6–10	10–15	15–20	6–15	15–20
Informal	6–8	8–10	10–10	10–15	15–20	20–25	10–20	20–25
Audiovisuals		6–8	8–12	12–16	16–20	20–25	16–20	20–25
PCs – General	4	6–8	8–10	10–14	14–18	18–27	14–18	18–27
PCs – CD-ROM		1–2	2–2	2–4	4–5	5–9	5–6	6–9
Multi-purpose Hall	~35	35–45	45–60	60–75	75–115	115–150	75–115	115–150
Shelf Space: 33 books x m	300	395–760	760–1090	1090–1515	1515–2120	2120–2725	1820–2425	2425–3335
CD Racks: 225 CD/60x90 cm unit		5–7	7–10	10–13	13–17	17–25	15–20	20–30

Update of IFLA Manifesto

"10 ways to make a public library work / Update your libraries".

Public library principles are the foundation of the UNESCO Public Library Manifesto 1994. This manifesto is a universal framework which expresses the general aims that public libraries should follow and the services that must be developed to provide universal access to global information.

IFLA and UNESCO understand that libraries and municipal governments need guidelines to help standardise the implementation of the Manifesto. IFLA Sections have worked to provide several guidelines including recommendations, best practices and standards to improve library services.

Over the last few years, several guidelines have been published as follows:

- *The IFLA/UNESCO Public Library Manifesto.* IFLA. 1994.
  http://www.ifla.org/VII/s8/unesco/eng.htm
- *The Public Library Service: IFLA/UNESCO guidelines for development.* IFLA Publications 97. Munchen, Germany. Saur 2001. ISBN 3-598-21827-3.
  http://www.ifla.org/VII/s8/proj/publ97.pdf

The IFLA Public Library Section in 2009 have now produced some additional recommendations to supplement the manifesto so that public libraries can place their services in the 21st century with use of the new technologies which have become available since 1994.

We hope that you will share with us the conviction that our public libraries have a relevant role in the developing world of Internet and digital provision. Our skills will have to be continually developed and enhanced but we believe that the degree of success of the public library and its role with these technologies in the next few years will be determined as the key to opening the gateway of a new global community.

We have to be "brave" and propose new ideas to improve our libraries services.

1. Develop public library buildings with the emphasis as community/cultural spaces not just physical stores of knowledge.
2. Liberate our services using the World Wide Web and Web 2.0, and look towards Web 3.0 and 4.0.
3. Connect with our communities and educate and train people where required. Librarians and Information Scientists can act as educators and personal knowledge advisors and not just keepers of keys or Internet gatekeepers.
4. Develop a "world wide wisdom" – a global knowledge and understanding by creating international cultural pathways on the web.
5. Work internationally to erode barriers and censorship whilst respecting all cultures.
6. Support our staff with continued training and encouragement to be proactive.
7. Develop our digitised collections services and knowledge – the hybrid library – knowledge, education and information in diverse forms.
8. Improve accessibility to our catalogues and databases especially for users with visual impairments.
9. Establish national and international standards on the Internet environment.
10. Public libraries as cultural storehouses – the "live" environment alongside the "recorded" one – archives, museums, libraries and culture combined: a "comby library".

IFLA Public Libraries Section. 2009.

Appendix 6

Queensland Standards and Guidelines for Public Libraries

Queensland Standards and Guidelines for Public Libraries
http://www.slq.qld.gov.au/info/publib/policy/guidelines

1. Library management standards – To provide the community with a library service that is equitable, cost effective and efficient.

2. Staffing standard – To provide the minimum requirement for overall staffing and qualified staff levels to ensure consistency of service delivery across local government. Revised May 2008.

3. Operational Services Standard – To provide standards and guidelines for a minimum set of operational services that enable the community effective access to library facilities and the services and collections they offer. Revised August 2009.

4. Library Buildings Standard – To provide standards and guidelines for developing physical library facilities which serve the identified needs of the community. Library buildings should be attractive and designed for efficiency, sustainability, accessibility, functionality and flexibility. Revised October 2009.

5. Mobile libraries standard – To provide standards and guidelines for a public library service delivered via a specially designed and equipped vehicle. Mobile libraries extend library service to clients without convenient access to a static library, providing a comparable level of service. Revised June 2009.

6. Library collections standard – To provide standards and guidelines for the development and management of library collections which meet the information, education, recreation and cultural needs of the community, and support the development of lifelong learning. Revised June 2009.

7. Interlibrary loans standards – To facilitate access by the local community to resources held in other Australian library and information services collections.

8. Local studies collection standards – To maintain or provide access to a collection which documents the historical development of the local community.

9. Reference Services Standard – To provide standards and guidelines for the delivery of effective reference and information services to the community and the collection and management of suitable resources to support these services. Revised October 2009.

10. Specialist service standards – The following sub-sections address a range of possible specialisations within the public library sector. They address the library's focus on literacy issues, services for people who read or speak a language other than English, in addition to addressing services for people with a disability, for young people and for Indigenous Australians.

    To meet the different emphases of different communities including unidentified groups, consideration of specialisation must be considered in the context of the mainstreaming of resources and multiskilling with the overarching principles of equity and access routinely applied.

    10.1 Literacy service standards – To actively promote and support programmes for members of the community with identified literacy needs.

    10.2 Multicultural services standard – To provide standards and guidelines for developing multicultural library services which provide equitable access, encourage participation and foster cohesion for Queensland's culturally and linguistically diverse communities. Revised July 2008.

    10.3 Disability services standard – To provide standards and guidelines for developing library services and resources which offer barrier-free access and encourage inclusiveness and participation for people with disabilities. Revised April 2009.

    10.4 Young peoples services standard – To provide standards and guidelines for developing young peoples services in libraries. Revised April 2009.

    10.5 Library services for Aboriginal People and Torres Strait Islanders standards – To actively consult and negotiate with Aboriginal and Torres Strait Islander peoples to promote library and information literacy and to catalyse the development of public library services. Draft standard currently under review.

11. Technology standard – To provide a framework for the efficient and effective use of technology as an integral feature of the public library so that optimum service can be provided. To provide all library sites, staff and users access to technology as required. Revised December 2008.

12. Resource Description standard – To provide a framework for access to library collections, through the bibliographic control of library materials and the interchange of bibliographic data. Revised October 2008.

13. Shared Facilities standard – To provide the minimum requirements for operating a public library service within a shared environment. Revised December 2008.
    - Guidelines and Toolkit for Shared Facilities best practice – December 2008.
14. Standards for Country Lending Service libraries – The basic requirements for the operation of a library within the Country Lending Service are prescribed by the Country Lending Service Agreement made between participating Local Governments and the Library Board of Queensland. The Agreement outlines the responsibilities of both parties. The following standards are based on the general provisions of the Agreement. Revised July 2004.

Appendix one – Bibliography
Appendix two – ALIA policy statements

General IFLA Resource List

IFLA manifestos

IFLA. (1995). *IFLA/UNESCO Public Library Manifesto*, The Hague: IFLA. (http://www.ifla.org/VII/s8/unesco/manif.htm)

IFLA. (1999). *IFLA/UNESCO School Library Manifesto*. (http://www.ifla.org/en/publications/iflaunesco-school-library-manifesto-1999)

IFLA. (2002). *The IFLA Internet Manifesto*. (http://www.ifla.org/publications/the-ifla-internet-manifesto)

IFLA standards and guidelines

Cylke, F., Byrne, W., Fiddler, H., Zharkov, S.S., and IFLA Section of Libraries for the Blind, Standards Development Committee. (1983). *Approved recommendations on working out national standards of library services for the blind*. The Hague: IFLA, 1983.

Day, J.M., and IFLA Section for Libraries Serving Disadvantaged Persons. (2000). *Guidelines for library services to deaf people*, 2nd ed. Professional report #62. The Hague: IFLA.

IFLA Libraries for Children and Young Adults Section. (2003). *Guidelines for Children's Libraries Services*. The Hague: IFLA. (http://www.ifla.org/en/publications/guidelines-for-childrens-library-services)

IFLA Libraries for Children and Young Adults Section. (2007). *The Guidelines for Library Services to Babies and Toddlers*. The Hague: IFLA. (http://archive.ifla.org/VII/d3/pub/Profrep100.pdf)

IFLA Section for Library Services to Multicultural Populations. (2009). *Multicultural communities: guidelines for library services*, 3rd ed. The Hague: IFLA. (http://www.ifla.org/en/publications/multicultural-communities-guidelines-for-library-services-3rd-edition)

IFLA Section of Public Libraries. (1998). *The public library as the gateway to the information society: the revision of the IFLA guidelines for public libraries, proceedings of the IFLA/UNESCO Pre-Conference Seminar on Public Libraries, 1997*. The Hague: IFLA.

Kavanaugh, R., Sköld, B.C., and IFLA Section of Libraries Serving Persons with Print Disabilities. (2005). *Libraries for the blind in the information age : Guidelines for development.* The Hague: IFLA.
(http://www.ifla.org/en/publications/ifla-professional-reports-86)

Lehmann, V., Locke, J., and IFLA Section for Libraries Serving Disadvantaged Persons. (2005). *Guidelines for library services to prisoners,* 3rd ed. Professional report #34. The Hague: IFLA.
(http://archive.ifla.org/VII/s9/nd1/iflapr-92.pdf)

Muller, P., Chew, I., and IFLA Section of Libraries for Children and Young Adults. (2008). *Guidelines for Library Services for Young Adults* The Hague: IFLA.
(http://www.ifla.org/en/publications/revised-guidelines-for-library-services-for-young-adults) ch 3

Nielsen, G. S., Irvall, B., and IFLA Section of Libraries for Disadvantaged Persons. (2001). *Guidelines for library services to persons with dyslexia.* The Hague: IFLA. (http://archive.ifla.org/IV/ifla72/papers/101-Nielsen-en.pdf)

Panella, N.M., and IFLA Section for Libraries Serving Disadvantaged Persons. (2000). *Guidelines for libraries serving hospital patients and the elderly and disabled in long-term care facilities.* Professional report #61. The Hague: IFLA.
(http://archive.ifla.org/VII/s9/nd1/iflapr-61e.pdf)

Pestell, R., and IFLA Mobile Libraries Round Table. (1991). *Mobile library guidelines.* Professional report #28. The Hague: IFLA.

IFLA reports

IFLA. (n.d.) *The IFLA/UNESCO Multicultural Library Manifesto.*
(http://www.ifla.org/en/publications/iflaunesco-multicultural-library-manifesto)

IFLA. (n.d.) *Professional codes of ethics for librarians.*
(http://www.ifla.org/en/faife/professional-codes-of-ethics-for-librarians)

IFLA Public Libraries Section. (n.d.) *Acts on library services.*
(http://www.ifla.org/V/cdoc/acts.htm)

IFLA Public Libraries Section. (2008). *Meeting User Needs: A checklist for best practice produced by section 8 – public libraries section of IFLA.*
(http://www.ifla.org/VII/s8/proj/Mtg_UN-Checklist.pdf)

IFLA Section for Public Libraries. (2003) *The Role of Libraries in Lifelong Learning. Final report of the IFLA project under the Section of Public Libraries*
(http://www.ifla.org/en/publications/the-role-of-libraries-in-lifelong-learning)

IFLA Section of School Libraries and Resource Centers. (2002). *The IFLA/ UNESCO School Library Guidelines 2002.*
(http://www.ifla.org/en/publications/the-iflaunesco-school-library-guidelines-2002)

Yarrow, A., Clubb, B., Draper, J., and IFLA Public Libraries Section. (2008). *Public Libraries, Archives and Museums: Trends in Collaboration and Cooperation.* Professional reports, #108. The Hague: IFLA. (http://www.ifla.org/en/publications/ifla-professional-reports-108)

Index